EVANGELICAL CHRISTIANITY:

REMOVING THE ANCIENT BOUNDARY STONES

AN URGENT APPEAL FOR A RETURN TO BIBLICAL CHRISTIANITY

By Dean Stevenson

Text Copyright © 2022 Dean Stevenson
All Rights Reserved

All bible quotations are taken from the Authorised King James Version of the bible unless otherwise stated.

Picture "Joan of Arc's Death at the Stake" by Hermann Anton Stilke (1803-1860)

An example of making the ultimate sacrifice in fighting against corruption, lies and deceit

"Remove not the ancient landmark, which thy Fathers have set."
(Proverbs 22:28)

Dean as been a Christian for over 30 years and in that time has experienced every possible hue of the Church spectrum, creeds and culture. He has travelled extensively throughout the UK, across Europe and as far as the Philippines visiting many congregations from the Highlands of Scotland to churches on the Southern Island of the Philippines on Mindanao, all the while documenting his experiences and conversations in his numerous journals.

He has served as a Deacon in two of his local churches and has also previously enjoyed being the editor and contributor of a local church newsletter submitting numerous articles. He has also self published a number of leaflets and booklets for local and evangelistic use, and has had two poems published in a Lancashire book of poetry. More recently he has had the wonderful privilege to have been used in a local preaching ministry for a number of years in East Lancashire preaching in local churches.

Dean works full time in the NHS as a front-line worker and is married to Michelle. He lives with his wife in the small village of Salterforth, Lancashire, England, UK. This is his first dip into the e-book world and is currently working on other projects for future publication. He is hoping to bring 30 years of Christian life experience and 55 years of 'general' life experience to bear in this his first small volume.

This book is dedicated to all the people that God has brought across my path, both Christian and non-Christian who have enriched my life with both positive and negative experiences by the sovereign overruling hand of Almighty God. May it be taken and used by the Lord Jesus Christ for His own eternal glory. Amen

Contents:

Introduction

Chapter 1....Ancient Landmark One: A Reliable Translation of the Scriptures..Page 16

Chapter 2....Ancient Landmark Two: Continue Preaching..Page 34

Chapter 3....Why We Should Believe the Entire of the Old Testament..Page 51

Chapter 4....A Warning: Handle God's Word Faithfully..Page 67

Chapter 5....Time for a Honest, Biblical Self Examination.. Page 80

Chapter 6....A Short Interlude and Summary..............Page 103

Chapter 7....Getting Back Our Zeal and Contending for the Faith..Page 108

Chapter 8....A Christian Response to the Laws of the State When in Contradiction to the Law and Will of God.....Page 135

Chapter 9....Apologia and Final Thoughts....................Page 152

"In those days there was no king in Israel: Every man did that which was right in his own eyes."
(Judges 21:25)

Introduction
It has been said by many in our day that we now live in a "Post-Truth" culture. Whatever we think that means or doesn't mean it does reveal two very interesting things: number one, the statement is a clear acknowledgement and confession that true truth and moral absolutes do actually exist, and secondly it is an equally clear confession that we are currently living in a culture of lies, deceit and deception. Truth 'used' to exist, now truth is relative, it's movable, it's whatever you want it to be, for instance yesterday I identified as a man, today I identify as a woman, the physical, biological, genetic and scientific reality and truth mean nothing. Truth does not necessarily need to be an absolute, it can and does change. Morality used to be 'a thing', now we exist in an amoral universe "doing that which is right in our own eyes." What some have labelled the "Judeo-Christian" world view was the former culture in which we lived, that culture, our western culture can now be said to resemble Ezekiel's "valley of dry bones", for everywhere we look (from that Judeo-Christian perspective) there is political and moral disease; there is pollution and decay; there is corruption, vileness and lies. Indeed every aspect of our lived-in existence and experience, from the womb to the grave has within it and around about it the "Post-Truth" world-view.

A clear example of this is the old view of marriage and the family. Marriage was once honoured, it was seen as the best environment to raise children and a family; it was seen as between one man and one woman committed for life, "until death do us part." What do we have now? What is the overwhelming and prevailing world-view upon marriage, children and the family? Well, non could argue against the fact that it is now a totally opposite world-view. Sleep with who you like, marry or don't marry, that's up to you, male or female, that doesn't matter and for many the concept of male and female doesn't even exist. If a women does get pregnant she can, at her own will kill the unborn child, her freedom to choose life or death is enshrined in law. The biblical view on marriage, gender, sexuality and the family is completely rejected and actually seen as harmful by many. What a turn around. This is just one example of what a shift in a cultural world-view looks like. When one begins to look at how we educate our children and with what we educate them, how we run and organise our families and communities, how our judicial systems operate and what laws are being passed, how our political systems function, how we deal with national, international and global decision making, who we do our trade with, and with whom we refuse that same trade, who we impose sanctions upon and of course who we choose to go to war with. I would put it to you that we deal in all these areas and much more with far less honour and truth than we used to, and that's putting it mildly!

All the mechanisms to protect this "New World Order" of a "Post-Truth" culture are also enshrined in domestic and international laws, and those who dare to resist or expose the systems do so at their peril, for they stand the very real possibility of being completely "cancelled" and destroyed all together. Hate crime laws, company "policies and procedures", "protected characteristics" are the very things being used to silence the dissenters, those who dare to believe in a different narrative or who hold an opposite world-view. Global governments, the United Nations, The World Health Organisation, mainstream media, big tech and social media are all working together to give us (for our health and well-being of course) a globally controlled existence that cannot be opposed.

Francis Schaeffer (1912-1984) a Christian Pastor and Apologists spoke and wrote of this changing culture and the influence it would have in every aspect of our lives. He understood completely that the world was changing and that the 20th century was a century like non other that had gone before it. Technology was changing everything, and when this technology is added to a fast changing culture, from a Judeo-Christian one to a Post-Truth one then the outcome would be catastrophic indeed. Of course there is "nothing new under the sun" as Solomon teaches us, but it is the technology that brings all that has gone before, and all that's ever existed into every home, into every ear and into every eye. There is literally no getting away from it. Total depravity is everywhere, it is a Tsunami of pollution and a deluge deception. Schaeffer spoke of the arts, music, film and television and the media (he died before the internet took hold). He spoke of these things not because he wanted to be some kind of social reformer but because he understood about the negative influence that would prevail in a post-truth world. The mediums mentioned above along with the internet in the hands of the devil and his disciples totally manipulates and influences our very thinking and behaviour, it deceives and desensitises, it numbs the conscience and makes millions believe in and worship him. This is like the devil in Revelation chapter 12 when he spewed water from his mouth to carry away the woman (The Church), or like when Satan is loosed from the bottomless pit to once again deceive the nations. (Rev.12:13-15, ch.20:1-3,7-8). This is the scale of what we are facing, and this is the reality of our times.

This little book is about the influence that has prevailed upon the church, upon individuals, upon the pastors and leaders in our churches. As the world (particularly the Western culture) has moved away from an influence of Christian thought upon it, the world has returned the favour and influenced the church to move away from its own foundational moorings, and we have gladly acquiesced. The verse of scripture that heads this chapter pretty much sums up the predominant thinking in our churches. We profess to have Jesus as our King but it is evident that he is not king of our lives let alone king over our churches. "There is no king in Israel" and subsequently "every man (and woman) does that which is right in their own eyes." In Israel at that time a kind of spiritual anarchy prevailed throughout the land and a simple read through the book of Judges reveals just that. The king of any nation in those days would have been responsible for making sure the rule of law was being kept and that no rebellions were being planned; insurrection and lawlessness was dealt with strongly and swiftly. Jesus is our lawgiver as well as our saviour; he is our Lord and King, and the Father has "delivered us from the power of darkness, and hath translated us into the kingdom of his dear Son." (Colossians 1:13). We are now in the realm of The Kingdom of God, we have a new King over us, we have new laws and we should have a new heart, new desires and a new principle of life of obedience, holiness, thankfulness and giving glory to God. This is "The New Birth" as 2 Corinthians 5:17 declares it, "therefore if any man be in Christ, he is a new creature: old things are passed away, behold all things are become new."

Having now become citizens of this new kingdom; and having now accepted the Lordship of our new King it naturally follows that we seek with all our hearts to advance the cause of Christ. But, it might be asked how are we to live our lives and how advance the kingdom of God? Well the simple answer is that God himself has provided and preserved a divine revelation for us and for our churches. It's all there "...precept upon precept;...line upon line; here a little and there a little." (Isaiah 28:10). Here we have a majestic testimony of divine truth, "knowing this first, that no prophecy of the scripture is of any private interpretation. For prophecy came not in old time by the will of man: but holy men of God spake as they were moved by the Holy Ghost," and by this process we received "a more sure word of prophecy." (2 Peter 1:19-21). Indeed "all scripture is given by inspiration of God, and is profitable for doctrine, for reproof, for correction, for instruction in righteousness: that the man of God may be perfect, throughly furnished unto all good works." (2 Timothy 3:16,17). The Word of God, the Bible is our rule book. There should be no spiritual anarchy in our churches nor by ourselves as individuals, we have all that we need "man shall not live by bread alone, but by every word of God." (Luke 4:4).

All this seems pretty simple and pretty straight forward does it not? We have a new kingdom and a new king; we have a beautiful, new revelation from our God revealing to us how we should order our lives and churches, and we have been granted new hearts, new minds and a new spirit, with new desires and new aspirations on how to live this new life. What could possibly go wrong? Well I will tell you what I believe has gone wrong and it is the only thing that could go wrong, it is that we have moved away from the solid rock of Jesus' words to "doing that which is right in our own eyes." Once that simple move is made then the results will be absolutely catastrophic, this cannot be overstated enough. A departure from God's word, a denial or a casting aside, however which way we want to put it can and will only end in personal disaster and ecclesiastical destruction. If the devil can only get us to doubt God's Word, or deny God's Word, or cause us to question and rationalise around the revealed truth then both we as individuals and the church will completely lose our authority, our power, our purpose, and we shall have no meaningful message at all; we shall be like a ship with no rudder or sails tossed about on the open sea. The post-truth cultural influence has prevailed upon us, science, liberal theology and technology has all undermined our evangelical position; we have doubted and we have drunk from the cup of the present cultural poison.

When the Lord God created all things and when it was all completed in it's beauty, harmony, complexity and glory with mankind, male and female at it's pinnacle, then the devils first and initial attack was to put doubt and disobedience to God's Word into the minds of our first parents. He knew that if he succeeded at this single point then the whole thing would begin to collapse, relationships would be destroyed and death and destruction would reign. God is a God of order, peace and harmony. He creates and desires balance, order, form and beauty; he is indeed the true and original artist. The devil on the other hand is the polar opposite in all his deceptive and diabolical nature. His first aim in the garden of Eden was to create disorder, confusion and doubt; he was to engender corruption and division, and with those simple yet destructive words "Yea, hath God said...?" (Genesis 3:1) he would begin a maelstrom of such death and decay that only the death of God's own Son and his miraculous resurrection could reverse.

Brothers and sisters in the Lord, this is exactly where the devil has succeeded. That catastrophic influence of a seismic shift in our culture spoken of by Schaeffer and others has happened and is a reality. The church universal simply failed to deal with it, heed the warnings or even see it coming. Through this shift and influence within those global technological mediums the devil has caused an almost mass weakness and confusion amongst God's people. We have drifted away from our past moorings, we have begun to build upon the sand and our past fundamentals once held dear are seen as teachings of an ancient bygone age, traditional, old fashioned and dead. People who profess to have experienced being born-again by God's Holy Spirit and to have met with Jesus; people who profess to have been saved etc. these very same people struggle to believe in the 6 Day Creation, doubt the global flood, side-step the destruction of Sodom and Gomorrah and the reasons for its demise, overlook the Lord's dealings in judgement with Israel, simply do not understand the life, death and resurrection of our Lord Jesus and the implications for them, care not for the commandments of God nor how the church should be operating, or who should be leading/preaching and who should not be leading/preaching. Many churches have replaced all this doubt and denial in the scriptures with activity and entertainment. "It's all about Jesus, I just care about him, he is all that matters and I don't let myself get bogged down with all that divisive doctrine, we shouldn't judge." These are the type of statements I have received on a numerous of occasions from elders, deacons, vicars (male and female) and pastors as well as the rank and file of brothers and sisters in the Lord. Truly the truth has been sacrificed on the alter of appeasement to the secular god of culture.

Iron used to sharpen iron, (Proverbs 27:17) and they that loved and feared the Lord spoke often with one another (Malachi 3:16). Nowadays many are too easily offended and care not of conversations about Jesus, the real, scriptural Jesus that is! The age of the spiritual snowflake is upon us with many Christians so easily upset and unable even to listen to the truth and unable even to debate certain issues, but rather melt away at the slightest confrontation. The church has, I believe, imbibed the spirit of the age and has become weak and worldly, secular and carnal. But, how can we combat these problems? What is needed at this time? How can this situation be reversed? These and many other such like questions have flooded my mind for many years and this little book I believe is what God has laid upon my heart and shown me some of the answers to those questions.

We could discuss the 6 day creation or God's eternal judgement or whatever biblical subject, but I wish to go back before that debate even takes place. I have sought to strip everything back to the bare bones, to go right back to the fundamentals and the essentials, to the very ancient landmarks which have been removed. Think, my friend of the reformers, they had before them a whole continent steeped in superstition, confusion, fear, guilt and sin; they also had to face head on a corrupted, polluted, abominable and fierce Roman Catholic Church system which would burn to death any who challenged it's authority. What did God do to bring this all system down? What did the Lord tell these men was the best course of action? What saved millions across the continent from their superstition and sin? And both of these points are extremely important, quite simply it was firstly, a return to the proper preaching of the word of God and secondly, making sure that the people had in their own hands a reliable, faithful translation of the scriptures in their own languages. These were the first ancient landmarks which had been removed by the Catholic system which the reformers sought to replace and to build upon. It is right here where the Reformers began their invaluable work, and it is right here that we also must begin our work.

What I have to say here upon these subjects is not as exhaustive or perhaps as in-depth as other writers, indeed I realise whole books could be written on each chapter, but I wanted to be as concise as possible, giving just an overview of the subject matter contained herein. However, I trust that for some pastors, church leaders, evangelists, lay preachers or indeed any brothers and sisters in whose hands these humble offerings might chance to fall, lessons might be learned, a closer walk with God desired and Jesus glorified. May these few words be used in the hands of God to bless abundantly the dear people of God, and may these same people look beyond the errors contained herein, peel away the carnal skin to eat of the divine fruit. I would ask that you would forgive my poor grammar, sentence construction etc. I am certainly no academic (and this work is self published!) but I do believe that it's a message that the Lord our God would have to us hear at this moment in our ecclesiastical history as well as in our present societal context. The question came to the Prophet "can these bones live?" What looked a totally hopeless situation became a miraculous opportunity for God to reveal himself powerful and true and real; all that was needed was obedience on Ezekiel's part to prophesy, to speak, to declare the words that God instructed him to say, and he could stand back and see the salvation of the Lord: a nation raised from the dead. (Ezekiel ch. 37:1-14). The Reformers followed the same pattern and a whole continent (and beyond) was completely transformed by the power of God. What looked unassailable, what looked impossible and what looked beyond hope became the miracle of the Reformation. Let us look therefore at the pattern they followed, which was the biblical pattern, true truth, absolute, unchanging and of Divine origin.

"For the time is come that judgement must begin at the house of God: and if it first begin at us, what shall the end be of those who obey not the gospel?" (1 Peter 4:17).

Yours, ever and always in the Lord

Dean Stevenson

Ancient Landmark One: A Reliable Translation

> "I will...praise Thy name for Thy loving kindness and for Thy truth: For Thou hast magnified Thy word above all Thy name."
> (Psalm 138:2)

> "It came to pass that when Jehudi had read three or four leaves, he cut it with the penknife, and caste it into the fire..."
> (Jeremiah 36:23)

You might be thinking that this subject is the very last thing that we need to be bothering with in our day, with all this chaos in the world, and with one seemingly global catastrophic event rolling into the next. Why indeed would I think that this will have any bearing whatsoever upon a blind, ignorant and dead world with all the sins, trouble, pain, heartache and suffering that unsaved people are caught up in? We really do not need to be dealing with this controversial and divisive subject now!

Firstly, though I understand those sentiments, I would however urge you to consider what I would propose in these next few pages as at the very least a starting point if we have any thoughts on reforming our churches and personal lives, which shall in turn be the best and most powerful blessing to the unconverted. This is about raising the bar which I believe has not only slipped but is completely broken; this is about honouring God and seeking out the best and being the best that we can. Think of Aquila and Priscilla after hearing Apollos preach the word of God they then took him to one side and "expounded unto him the way of God more perfectly." (Acts 18:26). Apollos was doing well, he was fervent and powerful but he lacked something and he was wrong about something, and it was Aquila with his wife Priscilla that encouraged him in his understanding of the Gospel. He was not too proud to listen to that humble couple, though he himself was "an eloquent man and mighty in the scriptures." (Acts 18:24). There are no doubt many more eloquent men and much more mightier in the scriptures than I, but I simply ask a hearing upon this issue.

Secondly, I am not directing these thoughts to the unconverted, rather towards the church, the congregations and church leaders, the preachers and pastors etc. What I am seeking to put forward is the fact that we have caste off the best of translations and replaced them with very weak and blasphemous paraphrases. What I am trying to suggest is that if we want to do the best by lost souls around us then is it not our responsibility before God to offer the finest gold and the finest jewels? The unbeliever knows no better, it is not his or her concern, I agree, but it most definitely is ours. In many areas of life we depend upon others who have greater understanding than us like doctors and surgeons for instance, they should be the experts and usually they are, and they are the ones entrusted to save our lives and they should know best. We do not need to know all that they know, but it is absolutely their responsibility to be continually researching their field of expertise; it is absolutely their responsibility to be using the best tools at their disposal, investigating the latest medical advancements etc. for the best outcome for the patient. The pastor is the spiritual surgeon, he is entrusted with souls, the world does not need to know what he should be an expert in, namely The Word God. But let us continue.

High or Low?
The above quoted texts of scripture show clearly two polar opposite views concerning the word of God. Firstly, we have an astonishingly high view of divine truth, and secondly, we have an extremely low view of divine revelation. God himself has declared that his word is of such high importance that he

rates it even above his own name! He has indeed magnified it above all his name; he has lifted it up; he has glorified it, it is raised up above all things in his created universe, and it is for this simple reason that translation matters, it absolutely matters. If God holds such a reverential view of his revelation to mankind then should not we? This is just the starting point of this discussion. Many Pastors, Christian leaders and biblical scholars have a very different view, they have a view like Jehudi; they have a very low view of the words of God. They do not care about the bibles they preach from; they do not care what bibles the flock in their care read from; they are not interested in trying to seek out and search the best translations, they think that they know best by human reasoning and they are not afraid to take a metaphorical penknife to the divine revelation which they hold in their hands. Not only do they think that this is of no concern whatsoever to the modern church but they actively and consistently avoid to teach the dear people of God many truths contained in God's word.

Whether we have high views or low views on the scriptures informs any further discussion. This most definitely is of such a fundamental necessity to the church, and it really is the first responsibility of the leaders to the people that God has entrusted them with to make sure that what he preaches from and what they themselves read is a reliable and trustworthy translation. If indeed he claims to be called of God then this must be his starting point. People coming into the church and getting saved really know no better, they are trusting that the gathering they come into is sound, biblical and built upon the Rock. If they imbibe liberal and careless attitudes regarding the word of God at this point then disaster will follow very soon; they themselves shall be worldly, carnal and careless; they themselves will be blind and ignorant because they have been led by the blind and the ignorant; they themselves will show very little fruit and any hungering and thirsting for

Christ and holiness will very soon diminish away and they themselves shall finally become easy prey for the devil who is seeking to ruin their lives. Remember when Jesus was being tempted of the devil in the wilderness, he could reply "It is written..It is written..It is written." (Luke 4:4,8,10). Pastors with such low views of God's words cannot say this neither can their flock. Doubt and confusion reigns in the lives of these 'penknife pastors' which is passed onto their congregations. Alternatively, those pastors and church leaders with higher views of the word of God will care deeply and with a passion which translation they have in theirs and their hearers hands; they will understand that it matters a great deal and that they have no authority whatsoever to add to or to take away from the revelation of the Lord. Indeed they will feel themselves cursed if they should play fast and loose with the scriptures as the last verses in the Book of The Revelation indicates, and because the Lord has raised his word so highly so too will they.

One more point which I wish to mention here but will deal with later on in the book is the fact that Jesus, our saviour and Messiah is called "The Word of God", and he said of himself that he is "the Way, the Truth and the Life," he also called himself "The Bread of Life". These are all terminologies and testimonies that reveal that Jesus and the Word are one! It naturally follows that he who has low views of the word; he who would dare to take his penknife to the scriptures; he who cares not one bit about getting the best translation to preach from or into the hands of the congregations; he who would avoid preaching upon certain subjects has indeed a very low and blasphemous view of Christ himself. To hold such views and be in the church as some type of leader is to be in a very precarious position indeed. But let us continue.

Order or Confusion?

How has this low view entered the assemblies of God's people? And how have the pastors, leaders and teachers of the scriptures imbibed such liberal ideas? As I stated, I believe that there has been a moving away from the bible as being the 'go to' reference point for all that we think, believe and act. And I also believe that it has been the devil's foremost aim to engender this confusion, doubt and departure, and one major way that he has achieved this is to pollute the scriptures themselves and to corrupt the English translations of the scriptures. I know and realise that this is not a particular popular subject, but I believe that it is the very place that we must start. This is exactly where the Reformers started and so too must we. The very fact that evangelicals today do not even think that this issue matters is proof in point of what I am proposing. Remember if we believe in God at all; if we profess to have been saved at all; if we testify of loving God and his Word at all then should it not concern us that God's own written, inspired, divinely authored Words matter? Of course they matter and to think otherwise reveals delusion has already set in. Today's Christians must understand or be freshly taught that we simply cannot play fast and loose with the word of God, these things really matter. It matters what words the Lord actually uses to reveal his mind and we are simply not at liberty to paraphrase the words of God. I myself had not been a Christian long when I started to come across differences in translations, in the notes in the margin it said things like "not in the original", "the oldest manuscripts (MSS) are missing x,y,z.", "Many MSS contain x,y,z." These statements are found on every page and nearly every chapter and they created in me a doubt regarding the veracity and preservation of the scriptures, how could they actually be trusted with such variants? Do we actually have the words of God in our hands or not? Is he able to preserve his own words or not?

Let us begin with the scriptures themselves, in other words what does our God say, "for God is not the author of confusion, but of peace, as in all churches of the saints" (1 Corinthians 14:33). It is not the will of God to engender confusion but peace, harmony, unity and oneness. The devil on the other hand is all about disunity, division, confusion and doubt. Again we have two polar opposite points of view, or will. God wills order, the devil desires disorder. I mention this because it is what we know about God and what we know about the devil which will help us to understand the direction we should be going, or the way we should be thinking upon this subject. If God's nature and character reveals that he is a God of order and harmony, and if we know that the devils character reveals that he desires to create doubt and division etc. then even before we get to discussions regarding textual criticism we realise that there is something not quite right about the English speaking world having a 120 (at the last count) current translations of the scriptures! That simple fact alone should set the alarm bells ringing, but ask yourself a simple question: would a 120 translations of the scriptures be likely to lead to order and harmony, or would it most likely lead to confusion and division? I think I know what the honest answer would be to that simple question, but if you have difficulty answering that question honestly then let me tell you that even in a church with just maybe 5 or 6 translations it is difficult enough when it comes to bible studies and when everybody is reading round and commenting from their own particular paraphrase. The very authority of God is brought into question and also the church, how could the church possibly preach or evangelise and take the scriptures into an unbelieving world when they differ so dramatically?

So, let us recap and remember our first foundational stone: Do we have a high view of God's revelation or a low one, and now our second foundational stone is: God is not the author of confusion, the devil is, and without doubt confusion reigns regarding these English translations. As a side point; how do you think that this looks to the unbelieving world? We have become a joke. God's words are one and we have made them 120! A handful of translations might be passable but the majority are a blasphemous affront to the Lord who has inspired his prophets and preserved his inspired Word. We have Women's Bibles, Young persons Bibles, Gender Neutral Bibles and a whole host of ridiculous paraphrase Bibles, and added to this a constant flow of revisions upon revisions continually changing the text. I have spoken with Muslims and Jehovah's Witnesses who have both said that the Christian Church has a hundred versions of the so called truth, and they are right. Before, we had One Bible and One Message, now we are babble of confusion with our scriptures and our evangelistic message. How can this possibly be of God? But, let us seek to answer the question, how has the devil succeeded in creating this mess?

Received Text or Critical Text?
As I stated earlier the evil one has been successful in disseminating corrupted texts and manuscripts from which have been translated the overwhelming majority of the English translations we have today. A great and terrible tragedy has occurred within Christendom and it is the wholesale acceptance of these modern translations and their corrupted texts coupled with a near total rejection of the Authorised King James Bible. Liberal and humanistic thinking has prevailed in our bible colleges and our pulpits and has for the most part persuaded the preacher and the people that these modern bibles are for the best. Most Christians do not even know what has happened or are even aware that there are indeed different manuscripts called The Critical Text and The Received Text. The simplistic arguments against the King James Bible like not understanding the Thee's and the Thou's have taken complete root and a total re-education of the

pastors and the people is needed with a subject that really we should not be dealing with, all this work has already been done by supremely better men than we shall ever be. The leaders in the church if they are called of God should already have a very high view of God's word and they should already realise that God is a God of order and not confusion, and consequently should themselves seek out and desire the best translation to both study for themselves, preach from and encourage their flock to read and study. However, let me give a short overview and then I shall recommend other sources for further investigation.

What is known as The Received Text or The Textus Receptus had always been used and always was the recognised preserved Texts for bible translation among the Christian Church since the church's inception up to the 1800's; that is for 1,800+ years! These were a gathering of collected manuscripts, copies and translations from the early church known as the Byzantine manuscripts because they came from that early church area, the area where the apostles and the church Fathers preached, established the churches and wrote their epistles. These manuscripts were always recognised as authoritative, reliable and moreover inspired, being copied from the original apostolic autographs. These manuscripts were also miraculously preserved. When the Islamic conquests began after AD600 and onwards these manuscripts found their way to Europe, into its universities and monasteries via Christians protecting them and fleeing the Muslim invaders. It was from these recognised Received Texts that eventually (after a few translation attempts) the Authorised King James Bible was translated. When these manuscripts were translated into the mother tongues of the European Continent the eyes of the people were opened and unprecedented reformation and revival swept across Europe, and from 1611 (the year of the King James translation) for the next 400 years or so the church and the English speaking world had One Bible. There were throughout this time many, many revivals and missionary endeavours with countless millions being converted across the globe. That's the good part!

As I said this all lasted up to the 1800's, but that century was indeed a year of devilish decline in many areas. This was the century of Darwins 'Origin of the Species'; this was the century of Higher Criticism in the churches advancing the bible denying cause of liberal theology. This was also the century that communism was invented by Marx (1818-1883), and the century Adolf Hitler was born and from him came Nazism. There were also a number of incredibly influential philosophers over this time Hegel (1770-1831), Schopenhauer (1788-1860), Kierkegaard (1813-1855) and Nietzsche (1844-1900), and later came Sartre (1905-1980). We could also add to this Freud (1856-1939). Why mention all these people? Well, we have to first understand the prevailing anti-Christian barrage that was engulfing the western world at that time. The impact of these people and many of the movements and ideologies that sprang out of them does have a bearing on our subject. Academia was under attack, the bible colleges were under attack; in fact the whole of western thought based upon Christian principles was under attack. It was all leading to an unprecedented move away from a general, if not an actual belief in the God of the bible. The idea of the ten commandments as good, and noble and wise; the concepts of moral good and real evil, of right and wrong etc. all of it was being questioned, denied and crushed.

All those movements had one thing in common they all denied the existence of God and denied the personal salvation of humankind through Jesus Christ. Or if they did profess to believe in God it was along-side their total rejection and denial of the miraculous and the Divine. They were theological liberals and paved the way for increasing denials and weakening in the fundamentals of the Christian Faith. Like I said in the introduction the culture was beginning to shift and it is here where it all began, the Judeo-Christian ethic was being replaced by a post-truth world view. This change in thinking cannot be brushed aside as insignificant. From out of these new ideas came 'Evolution' which bred a whole new anti-God science, as well as influencing directly Nazi ideology and the new Communism. Communism and Nazism together with the two World Wars was directly responsible for the deaths of millions upon millions.

It was in this context and into this academic background with all these direct influences upon them that two men Wescott and Hort desired to produce a brand new Greek manuscript. Now, this new Greek revision would not be based upon the recognised and preserved Received Text (The Textus Receptus) but upon just a handful of manuscripts, the codex Vaticanus from the library at Rome and the newly discovered Alexandrian manuscript by Tischendorf (1815-1874) the codex Sinaiticus. The codex Bezae was another manuscript used. All these were known as the Critical Texts and these were just the handful of manuscripts they used for their new translation. Now the point is this that these man hated the Textus Receptus and are on record in their personal writings and letters that this is the case. They were not even believers in the God of the Bible nor in the fact that God could preserve his word. So they had a very low view of the scriptures to say the least. The manuscripts they used were full of omissions, additions, substitutions, transpositions and modifications. Which basically means that they were rubbish! A more scholarly person would say they were clearly unreliable texts for the translation into the Greek and then the English, or any other language for that matter. Indeed these manuscripts differed from each other in nearly 6,000 places! They do actually serve one good purpose in the fact they make the Received Text and The Majority Texts appear all the more what they are: Authoritative, Reliable, Trustworthy and Inspired!

Now, just to give some numbers as regards the Received Text there are some 20,000 part manuscripts and some 4,000 full Greek Texts, and if we add to this full translations in different languages from the 2nd, 3rd, 4th, and 5th centuries. There are also Peschito Syriac, old Latin, two Egyptian from the 3rd and 4th century, the Vulgate, Gothic and Armenian and Ethiopian translations. What we also have to add to this voluminous evidence is the almost complete bible quoted in the Early Church Fathers known as the 'Patristic Citations.' These are equally important because those Early Church Fathers would have had the original autographs at their disposal, or at least very early copies, and their quotations reveal the authenticity of the actual Greek manuscripts, copies and translations already mentioned. What we have in these thousands of available manuscripts and texts to hand is near perfect agreement, this is The Received Text. Wescott and Hort totally rejected all of this evidence and instead from their liberal and unbelieving mindset chose those handful of Critical Texts wherein is massive difference and disagreement not only with the Received Text but also amongst themselves.

Now, because of the prevailing unbelief and apostasy of those days the Wescott and Hort's new Greek Text based upon those corrupted manuscripts became the texts upon which nearly all our modern version are now based upon. This is the great and terrible tragedy of the Christian Church in our day, for the evil one has succeeded in replacing the preserved English translation based upon the recognised Received Text with a polluted and adulterated version. This in turn has spawned well over a hundred English translations and paraphrases resulting in the present doctrinal confusion and ever increasing low view of the word of God. We really need to get back to having a reliable and trustworthy translation and this is a fundamental necessity if the church is to get back any semblance of authority, harmony, unity, order and true faith in the one, true and living God. I urge pastors, church leaders, Christians of every creed to begin to lay back down this foundational stone. This is not a call to the Authorised Version specifically (though I believe it still to be the best) but to a translation based upon the Received Text.

You might be asking are there any other English translation based upon the Received Text? Well, probably the best one available would be the New King James Bible. Other experts might know of a better one and might disagree with me but I would recommend having a King James Bible and a New King James Bible together, and I do believe that they compliment each other and have the authority, reliability, readability and inspiration and can be read and followed together from the pulpit, to the pew, to the home, and the unity of doctrine is maintained. If you are wondering if the bible you have in your hands is based upon the corrupted manuscripts then I will give you these simple texts to look at which will tell you otherwise. The first three are a direct attack upon the deity of Christ, the last one reveals the author and the architect of this confusion.

Micah 5:2 "But Thou Bethlehem Ephratah, though thou be little among the thousands of Judah, Yet out of Thee shall He come forth unto Me that is to be ruler in Israel; who's going forth have been from old, from everlasting."

As you can see this is a prophecy regarding the birth of Jesus in Bethlehem, but what we are quite clearly told is that this Messiah, this person and this Son of God is "from Everlasting." He has an eternal heritage, he is from everlasting, he goes back forever and forever; this is God the Son. Now if your translation says anything different like "from of ancient times" or "from ages past" or whatever else then it is from those polluted manuscripts, it's as simple as that, because "ancient times" or "ages past" is not eternal, everlasting and forever. Devilish doubt has been created by the Father of lies. (John 8:44)

1 Timothy 3:16 "Without controversy great is the mystery of godliness: God was manifest in the flesh."

Now here we have another attack upon the deity of Jesus. The Received Text clearly says that it is "God" himself that is revealed or manifested "in the Flesh." This is one of the key proof scriptures regarding the deity of Jesus. However, most modern English translations based upon those corrupted texts will say "**He** was revealed", or "**He** appeared in the Flesh." They completely remove the word God and replace it with He! The old Jehudi penknife is out again.

1 John 5:7 "There are three that bear record in heaven, the Father, the Word, and the Holy Ghost: and these three are one."

Again the deity of Christ and the trinity itself comes under attack (a bit of a pattern forming don't you think). All translations based upon the polluted texts remove this verse altogether! If this verse is not in your bible then bin your bible, it's corrupted. This is the clearest statement of the divine trinity in the bible and would you believe it, it's gone, and who do you think might be behind such subtle tampering? There is no doubt about it, each passing translation and paraphrase will get worse and worse and further and further away from the original word of God.

Isaiah 14:12 "How art thou fallen from heaven, O Lucifer, son of the morning!"

If you asked anybody in world who Lucifer is I think nigh on 100% of the people would say "The Devil." Did you know that this is the only place where the name of the devil is given "Lucifer." Well, if your translation has removed the devils actual name then you have a corrupted bible based upon those Critical Texts. He who is responsible for all this adding and taking away, he has removed his own name to engender further confusion, because this text could quite easily mean some other king of Babylon and not the devil at all. Given a few generations where the name Lucifer is nowhere to be found millions will not be aware of who the devil is let alone the people of God. Even now many in our liberal churches deny the existence of a personal devil, saying that any mention in the scriptures is only figurative or purely symbolic. What a perfect crime to so influence the church that their most fiercest, dangerous and subtle of enemies doesn't even exist!

Accept or Reject?
I have sought to give an honest and short overview of how we got our AV bible and how we got our numerous other translations, and what manuscripts were used in the translation process. I have also put before your eyes just four very simple texts of scripture with very small, subtle changes, but these changes, especially the first three strike at the very heart of Christ himself and we need now to either accept or reject Christ because this is what this subject amounts to. Do you think that this does not matter? Is this of no concern to you? Is this all just a coincidence? If you have no concern to even pray about this situation and do some further research then I am afraid you are one who has a very, very low view of the scriptures indeed and you align yourself with all the Jehudi's of this world cutting up the word of God and throwing it into the fire. To even think that this issue is of no real importance is to believe that the Truth itself does not matter. Why are you in the job you are in if truth doesn't really matter? Where is your calling? Where is your sense of burden,

necessity, urgency? Your master demands higher from you, and you blaspheme his name by your low views of God's word. Remember, this is just the starting point of a return to our biblical roots: getting back into our pulpits and into our churches a reliable, trustworthy, inspired and preserved translation. Ask yourself another question, is the God who created a universe in 6 literal days not able to preserve his word? Also, would you think that the devil would not try and tamper and corrupt that testimony knowing his character? His very first temptation to Eve was "Yea, hath God said...?" (Genesis 3:1). Has God really said that? Does he really mean that? Can God really preserve his word? Are you completely sure about that? Doubt is the Devil's mistress and we join in with such spiritual fornication when we entertain low views of God and his word and doubt our Lord's ability to preserve his word.

As I said I have pointed out four simple changes, there are literally thousands of additions or omissions etc. which change entire meanings of texts and thoroughly alter doctrine. This isn't a situation where translators are trying to find the right word from similar meaning words, no, this is changing "God" to "He"; changing "everlasting" to "ancient times" and even missing out entire verses, or casting doubt on entire passages as in Mark 16:9-20 and John 7:53-chapter 8:11, the NIV placing these entire passages in italics as not in the original. When they say "not in the original manuscripts" what they really mean is "not in the Critical Text" from which Wescott and Hort used, all the other thousands of manuscripts, copies, translations (i.e. Received Text) and the Church Fathers quotations contain these verses. Incidentally, it's called The Critical Text for a reason!

You might be out there thinking that "I have one of those bibles which you say is corrupted and without a single doubt God has encouraged me, spoke to me and revealed Jesus to me, what about that if they are so bad?" I would say that God is merciful and will speak to his people with whatever they have in their hands. In the past some only had a new testament, others only a piece of parchment, and others had no bible at all! But God still spoke and God still saved. I am speaking of opportunity; if you have the opportunity for the best, then the best you should have. Having had the best in the past which knew remarkable, miraculous and evidential blessing the tragedy is that the church has cut it with the penknife and thrown it upon the fire. We have actually gone backwards and moved away from having the best and the finest translation and chosen a hundred or so translations and paraphrases to replace that one bible and thus created more confusion! It was the providence of God was it not that the "sun never set on the British Empire", and the best bible, the finest piece of literature that's ever graced any language was disseminated over the whole earth and only eternity will reveal the many millions of souls saved over all of those continents and continue to be so.

I am afraid I simply cannot do justice to this subject and in many ways I feel out of my depth but others do indeed deal with this subject in a much more brilliant way. There are tremendous resources available for those who's heart might have touched to re-evaluate their position whether they be pastor or church leader, or member of the congregation. Please consider prayerfully this important subject, this great foundational stone and ancient landmark which, I believe has been removed from many a church, bible college and many a heart. I urge you to raise your view of God's word to that of Psalm 138 "Thou hast magnified Thy word above all Thy [God's] name."

Let me finish this appeal again to those who wonder whether God has actually preserved a reliable set of manuscripts, Psalm 12 verses 6-7 declares emphatically "The words of the

Lord are pure words: as silver tried in a furnace of earth, purified seven times. Thou shalt keep them O Lord, Thou shalt **preserve** them from this generation for ever." What clearer testimony should we need. God is able to preserve his word and he has, it is The Textus Receptus: The Received Text. It is quite impossible for there to be two different bibles, you must accept the one and reject the other.

For further study please visit The Trinitarian Bible Society website at www.tbsbibles.org There you will find a fantastic selection of free PDF downloads on the history of the Received Text; how we got our English bible; who were the translators etc. etc. I have found these resources invaluable. Please try www.sermonaudio.com and type in the subject box "sermons on translations" for honest dealings with this subject by a variety of speakers. I found a nine sermon series by Dan Botterdrodt an absolutely tremendous help.

Also, I cannot recommend enough the book "The Revision Revised" by John William Burgon who delivers a scholarly critique of Wescott and Hort's Greek text and their use of those Critical Texts.

There are many, many other excellent books and sermons out there, please do avail yourself of the rich resources available. Again I urge you please do your research upon this critical subject. And let me just finally add just because some so called famous preacher whom you respect and admire, and who has even been a blessing to your soul uses an NIV or some other corrupted text do not let that hinder you from thinking for yourself and doing the right thing by weighing up the arguments and using for yourself the finest and the best which the Lord himself has preserved. Even famous preachers can have their blind spots!

Ancient Landmark Two: Continue Preaching?

> "Preach the Word, be instant in season, out of season; reprove, rebuke, exhort with all long suffering and doctrine. For the time will come when they will not endure sound doctrine...."
> (2 Timothy 4:2-3)

There is a growing tendency amongst 21st century 'snowflake' Christians to believe that preaching and teaching is becoming more and more ineffectual and somewhat negative to modern mankind. It is thought that we ought to be living the life of Christ as a witness rather than 'preaching at people'. It is also thought that in these days people are put off and will just switch off when some preacher is telling them what they ought to do. Modern Christians believe that because people and culture has changed, so too the church should change and be more fluid and flexible in it's activities and entertainment to influence and draw people in. Preaching (it is thought) is confrontational and aggressive, and really is of little use in modern society and the salvation of souls. Any preaching that's acceptable has become a like a glorified TED talk, or some slick 'power point' business presentation.

We have to ask are these thoughts and ideas correct? And given the apparent success of other churches who do less preaching in favour of activities should we not be following their lead? Is this the way that the church should be evolving in the 21st century: less preaching, doctrine and 'religion', but more activities, entertainment, social connections and/or business-like presentations?

If we are Christians at all then it is to the bible itself that we must go: "what saith the scriptures?" (Romans 4:3). This isn't just about going to a rule book to establish some ancient tradition or institution, but it is rather going to God's written word for God's mind and will upon any given situation or subject. It is about being humble and obedient to accept the simple truths of God himself. I have come to the conclusion that we must reject completely this modern cultural influence upon our churches and that the church simply must continue it's preaching and teaching ministry. This, I believe, can be easily understood and simply proved to those who have "ears to hear what the Spirit saith unto the churches." (Revelation 2:7).

Let me continue by stating that preaching is:

An Enduring Charge
Let us go to the text that heads this chapter. I urge you to read versus 1-5 of chapter 4. This is the apostle Paul speaking and he gives a most solemn and serious command to the young pastor Timothy. "I charge thee therefore before God and the Lord Jesus Christ, who shall judge the quick and the dead....Preach the Word!" Paul calls the God of heaven and our Lord Jesus himself as witness in this charge and command. He enforces the seriousness by saying that this is in light of the very judgement of God itself that he simply must "Preach the Word." This is serious stuff and not something that we can just take lightly. He continues, "be instant in season and out of season." This job must continue in the good times and in the bad times, when it is fruitful and when it is less fruitful, when people will listen and when they refuse to listen, when the culture is more Christian and when it is positively anti-Christian. "No matter what the situation Timothy" says Paul "Preach the word". Paul exhorts him of the nature of his preaching, it should involve reproving, convincing, exhorting, rebuking, and this should be done through doctrine (teaching) and with all long suffering and patience. There will be many uncomfortable and unpalatable things that he will have to say but he gives us the reason why it must be this way "for the time will come when they will not

endure sound doctrine; but after their own lust shall they heap up to themselves teachers, having itching ears; and they shall turn their ears away from the truth, and shall be turned unto fables. But watch thou in all things....do the work of an evangelist, make full proof of thy ministry." (verses 3-5). Quite simply he is to continue in this serious command because there will come times in the future when people will simply not want to hear God's word, "they will not endure sound doctrine,....they will turn their ears away from the truth" and believe rather what the culture says, what modern society says, what the scientist say and what the academics say.

We must ask are we in such days? Do we listen to culture and the complaints of the world rather than just obeying the Lord and continuing preaching and teaching God's word? Are we fearful of the new 'cancel culture' which can destroy anyone who opposes the 'New World Order' or the 'New Ecumenical Church Order' narrative?

But let us go on. If preaching is an enduring command it is also:

A Universal and Permanent Command
Preaching and teaching always was, it always is and always will be God's will and way in communicating the truth. God has made us creatures of language and communication. This is how we pass on ideas, plans, desires and aspirations etc. and this is how God communicates with us: through the spoken and written word. Remember, we are made in the image of God and Christ is called "the Word of God," and he says of himself "I am the Truth." And so it follows that God has always had his preachers, teachers and prophesiers, and always will have. In the book of Jude we read that "Enoch also, the seventh from Adam prophesied of these, saying Behold the Lord cometh with ten thousand of his saints, to execute judgement upon all..." (verse 14,15) What is important

to note here is that in those pre-flood days, the man who we are told was just the seventh direct descendant from Adam was a preacher! "Enoch....prophesied." He spoke clearly and strongly, warning the people in his day of the impending doom and forthcoming judgement of God. Culture meant nothing, and the hatred and violence of the days in which he lived meant nothing, he simply preached the word. Again, let us turn to another new testament text. In 2 Peter chapter 2:5 we are told quite clearly and simply that "Noah (was) a preacher of righteousness." Again, in those old times Noah was himself a preacher, a teacher or whatever you want to call him, and he was delivering the message of God to the people around at that time whom the Lord declares "that the wickedness of man was great in the earth...the thoughts of his heart were only evil continually...The earth also was corrupt before God, and the earth was filled with violence...for all flesh had corrupted his way upon the earth." (Genesis 6:5,11,12).

This was the state of the people at that time and what should be done about it? Well, before the judgements of a sovereign God fell upon them God had his preachers and prophesiers, we read of two men: Enoch and Noah, but I believe there would have been many more. The point being that at the beginning of the dawn of time God had his preachers and it did not matter what the culture was, it mattered not of the violence of those days or the world wide corruption or whether they listened or refused to listen, the command was the same and the charge remains the same, "Preach the Word!" The means that God used to communicate his way of salvation and warnings to flee the wrath to come did not change one iota. We could mention all those through the old and new testaments, all those Levite preachers, all those prophets, and all those apostles, teachers and pastors. No matter what the changing cultures brought forth over thousands of years and no matter whether the people were in times of peace and prosperity or whether they were in times of famine, sword, bondage and captivity, it was all the same: God had his preachers delivering his word and message. This is a universal and permanent charge and command: "Preach the Word, in season and out of season."

These really are very simple and basic truths contained throughout the scriptures and if our present generation had higher views of those scriptures then they would not entertain such secular concepts of influencing people or give credence to business models for church growth.

We have seen that the preaching and teaching ministry is universal, permanent and enduring, and we have mainly looked at those biblical times up to two thousand years ago, but let us consider for a moment the last two thousand years up to our point in history right now, in other words: the history of the church amid cultural changes.

Church History and Changing Culture
A cursory reading and understanding of church history will bring you to realise that God has always raised up and used preaching and teaching for the salvation of souls and for the building up of his people. This has been the case whether the church was in dark days or revival days, whether the world was making great scientific advancements or whether it was in a more stagnant state. The message of the gospel has never changed and neither has the means on how to communicate that message. When we think of the changes over the last two millennia what changes there have been! From the tribal savagery of the ancients world to the science-fiction and technological age that we now live in. From the old fearless explorers that sought to seek out new worlds through jungles and deserts, to our days of space travel. From the days of the axe, the sword and the hunter to the days of mobile communication devices and instant, transferable data. We could go on and on, but the point is this and I'm sure that you

would realise this, that the gospel and the word of God to this world (however advanced it might yet become) is always the same and the communication of that message is always the same: by the written and the spoken word.

Every single year since the days of the early church up until now Jesus has had his preachers and evangelists. Many names and their works are written in our history books and still many more are not. Throughout the globe the burdened soul winner and church planter has travelled prophesying through cities like Jonah or baptising in the wildernesses like John the Baptist, undeterred, unrelenting, driven by love and grace and the fiery Spirit of God. They have met with every possible nature of mankind, they have faced every possible culture known to man: High culture, Low culture or no culture at all. "Preach the word" burned in their hearts and drove them on fearing absolutely nothing but God and sin. These were no 'snowflake evangelicals' who melt at the least bit of mild confrontation; these were not spineless leaders like our current crop in the Church of England who are more interested in virtue signalling to every conceivable so called oppressed minority group. No, these were by the grace of God: Men of God. In and of themselves they might well have been weak and fearful, and they had their failures like Jacob, Moses, David, Peter and Paul, but they had a calling from God which forced them to caste themselves upon his mercy with agonising cries "God be merciful to me, a sinner," for "I can do all things through Christ which strengtheneth me." (Luke 18:13, Philippians 4:13). They embodied the spirit of the apostle Paul when he said "we preach not ourselves but Christ Jesus the Lord...but we have this treasure in earthen vessels, that the excellency of the power may be of God, and not of us. We are troubled on every side, yet not distressed; we are perplexed but not in despair; persecuted but not forsaken; caste down, but not destroyed." (2 Corinthians 4:5,7-9). Here we have a man who exemplified the very spirit of every preacher from his days up to now, facing every culture, every danger, every success and every failure, facing it with the Lord, preaching the same message in the same way to every nation, tribe, kindred and tongue.

One more important point that I would like to add here is that not only did the Lord have his preachers at the dawn of time, as we have seen with Enoch and Noah and not only has he raised up preachers and teachers throughout history and time, but also at the very end of the ages we see those who herald forth God's word no matter what cultural advancements there might be then. When we turn to the book of the Revelation, there we read in chapter 11 from verse 1-14 of two witnesses. Friends, at the end of the age God will have two prophets, two preachers, two evangelists and "they shall prophesy 1,260 days." (v.3) This is a very clear indication that The Lord desires the simple preaching of his word to continue for those days are not yet upon us! Whatever their message might be one thing is for sure the means to communicate that message will be the same. If we have our technology now, what will it be like then! But still the spoken word continues because this is God's way to communicate to people in whatever epoch of history they might be. Let not human reasoning, secular thinking or cultural changes be brought to bear upon our souls and minds, but rather let us stick to God's word and his means, whether we have so-called success or perceived failure, let one plant, let another water and God will give the increase.

Mankind and an Unchanging Nature
There is indeed a very good reason why the means and the message is the same and it is simply because mankind has not changed one 'iota', and our basic need of salvation by grace, through Jesus Christ has not changed either. This is a very simple truth that the modern Christian quite often forgets or perhaps doesn't understand or even believe. We somehow think that we are more cultured and more advanced and that

our needs have changed, and that we have somehow evolved to a kind of higher human being than those of centuries past. We tend to think that our young people are different from what we were or from those in the past, we think that their needs are different because the culture and age we live in is so different, and we therefore think that the preaching and teaching of the 'old school' will simply just not reach them at all, neither will it reach and change the advanced adult population. I am afraid that this is a terrible mistake, totally untrue and a complete lie of the devil himself.

The command of Paul to Timothy stands for all time to "do the work of an evangelist." (2 Timothy 4:5). To reach the masses the church must continue it's preaching and teaching ministry because mankind is no different in his real need from the dawn of time to the end of time. When you strip away the technology, when you strip away the space travel, the aeroplanes and the millionaire yachts. When you strip away the internet, the social media and the celebrity culture. When you strip away the music festivals, the holidays and the hedonism, when you strip away global governments, global trade and global empire building you are left with mankind absolutely exactly the same as fallen Adam and Eve naked and ashamed in the garden of Eden hiding from God. Our young peoples needs are no different whatsoever from Adam and Eve's first child Cain who was a murderer. Friends, the universal problem is sin, indwelling and original sin, this is the root cause of all our 'issues', and it is this problem that is met head-on in the preaching of the gospel. God has written and spoken into real-time history and he commands that we write and speak directly into our present cultural historical context. "Preach the Word" God commands it, no matter what the reaction might be, whether dismissive mocking or violence, whether we get success or apparent failure, whether thousands flock into the Ark of God's love and salvation, Jesus Christ, or whether just a few souls enter in. The growth and the fruit is not in our power, for it is "God that giveth the increase," (1 Corinthians 2:6). We are commanded to be faithful in preaching and teaching and leave the rest to the Lord, he alone can cause the spiritually dead to live. As I alluded to in my introduction the Lord asked the question to the prophet "...can these bones live?" the prophets reply is "O Lord God, Thou knowest." (Ezekiel 37:3). Ezekiel's job was then to obey the Lord , "...he said unto me prophesy unto these bones." (verse 4). We are duty bound to obedience and leave the results to God.

The day that Adam and Eve sinned they died, they died spiritually and lost communion with God. That 'Death' has thus been passed down upon all flesh and the divine record declares that we are "born in sin, shapen in iniquity." The Lord says that we are "ungodly, sinners and enemies", "dead in trespasses and sins", and that the "wrath of God abides over us" being "condemned already". (Psalm 51:5, Romans 5:6,8,10; Ephesians 2:1; John 3:18,36) Friends, we are hell-bound and dead and we are lost forever unless there is a way of escape. The point I wish to make here is that all our needs are the same, the culture that we are born in is completely irrelevant. Whether you live in a mud hut with barely any food to eat or whether you are of the "super rich" living in extreme opulence, God has designated that "there is none righteous, no not one... for all have sinned and have come short of the glory of God." (Romans 3:10,23). Our old people's needs are the same as our young peoples needs, men's needs are the same as women's needs, the rich person has the same spiritual poverty as the poor person, they all need to be made spiritually alive by God's Holy Spirit, and they all need to repent of their sins and believe the gospel. It is only a godless cultural influence that would suggest that we need a young persons bible, or a special women's bible, or even a gender neutral bible. If we understood the simple truth that we are indeed all the same with the same needs then we wouldn't be so easily brainwashed and manipulated with such nonsense. God has ordained the means for communicating his message to "all flesh" and it is the preaching and the teaching of the word of God throughout every age of mankind.

So we have seen that preaching is universal, enduring and permanent, and we have also seen that despite the culture, preaching is to continue because mankind's basic needs before God have not changed. We have been looking mainly at these issues from the unbelievers point of view and their needs, but what of the church? What of the people of God? What about teaching and preaching in the house of God? Again, some say that "they don't want preaching at" or that "doctrine doesn't matter, all that matters is knowing Jesus." How are we to answer those who feel that preaching carries a negative tone to it and that the modern Christian doesn't need it and just switches off?

Don't Throw the Baby Out with the Bath Water
Firstly, let me say that just because there might be some bad, negative, aggressive and condemnatory preaching that doesn't mean that we get rid of it all together and just because there might be weak, lifeless, powerless and liberal preaching that also doesn't mean that we caste it off as irrelevant. Again, I state that God's means for the up building and the establishing of the Christian church, corporately or individually has always been the same and will always be the same, and it is a consistent preaching and teaching ministry. In Ephesians 4 from verse 11-14 we are told that God "gave some apostles; and some prophets; and some evangelists; and some pastors and teachers, for the perfecting of the saints, for the work of the ministry, for the edifying of the body of Christ: Till we all come to a unity of faith, and of the knowledge of the Son of God, unto a perfect man...that we henceforth be no more tossed to and fro, and carried about by every wind of doctrine, by the sleight of men, and cunning craftiness,

whereby they lie in wait to deceive." (NKJV) This friends is a very important passage for it tells us a lot about what the preaching and teaching is all about in the church. Notice, Paul says that these gifts continue in the church until we reach perfection and unity, and a perfect knowledge of the Son of God (I don't think that we have reached that stage yet!). They continue also so that we might avoid those false teachers, and not be tossed about by their false doctrine. They also continue for the edifying of the body of Christ (the church). That word edifying means to be built up by knowledge, by teaching and by the word of God. This passage tells us plainly that this is to continue till the end of time. If we think that we do not need edifying or to be recipients of this work of the ministry, or if we think that we have somehow arrived at a complete unity of faith and a perfect knowledge of the Son of God, and if we think that we are now beyond the subtleties of those false teachers then I am afraid that we are sadly mistaken and are already taken captive by false teaching.

What of the modern idea "all that matters is Jesus, not doctrine?" Sadly, I have heard this a thousand times and it grieves my soul intensely, because it comes from the lips of those who should know better, from those who claim to know The Lord Jesus and to have been born anew. At first this might have an air of spirituality about it, but when looked at more closely we see that this idea is particularly dangerous and deceptive, and is anything but spiritual. This notion is often expressed in the light of what people say "we don't want 'religion', we want Jesus; we don't want 'doctrine', we want Jesus. Did not the Pharisees have plenty of 'religion' and plenty of 'doctrine' and look how they ended up?" How are we to answer these sentiments?

Firstly, the word 'doctrine' is not a dirty word, neither is it a negative term, it is simply another word for 'teaching'; they are synonymous terms and are to be used interchangeably.

And the liberal agenda within the Christian churches seeks to demonise doctrine and teaching by linking these terms with hypocrisy and Pharisaical dryness and deadness in Christianity: This indeed is a ploy of the devil himself.

Secondly, we must note and understand that true doctrine and true teaching when taught in truth and in the right manner cannot be separated from Jesus, they are one and the same thing. To explain this point more clearly let us turn to Luke chapter 24. In this passage we see the Lord Jesus rebuking the unbelief of those discouraged believers. They thought that Jesus was dead and that the whole thing was over. Christ himself came alongside them as they talked and "he said to them, O fools, and slow of heart to believe all that the prophets have spoken...And beginning at Moses and all the prophets, he expounded unto them in all the scriptures the things concerning himself." (verses 25-27). This is the point brethren, Jesus expounded, Jesus taught and Jesus used doctrines and teachings to reveal himself to them, they are one and the same. Jesus who taught the Word is himself the Word and he called them fools for not understanding this and for not seeing it. And what was their reaction? "And they said one to another, did not our hearts burn within us, while he talked with us by the way, and while he opened to us the scriptures?" (verse 32). This is not dry, dead doctrine; this is not 'religion'. Friends, when doctrine is rightly handled (which all preachers should attempt to do) it will be life and vitality; it will be fresh and relevant; it will be powerful and reviving; it will breathe faith into the peoples hearts and there will be divine power and divine anointing. In short it will be Christ Jesus revealed in the Word of God. This is not 'dead doctrine' or Jesus, this is heart-burning, faith-affirming and truth-confirming reality: this is God's way and means to save souls and to build up his people, and to suggest that Jesus and teaching are somehow separate is a serious and a grave error.

Another thing that we should consider is just because the Pharisees or anybody else for that matter might know the Word and yet not know Jesus does not mean that we should come to the conclusion that it is possible to know Jesus separated from the word of God. Jesus said to the Pharisees "Search the scriptures for in them ye think ye have eternal life, and they are they which testify of me." (John 5:39). If the Pharisees had understood the word of God by the Spirit they would have seen and known Jesus, for as Jesus said those very scriptures (which they knew back-to-front) testified of him and revealed him. Because they did not know or see him didn't mean that Jesus and doctrine are two different things. The problem was the lack of a work of the Holy Ghost in their hearts and lives and the birth of saving Faith. Jesus himself said that the Pharisees couldn't see him and he called them blind, and thus he says "their sin remaineth." (John 9:41).

Millions of people have bibles and read them but they do not see themselves nor the need of a saviour, neither do they see the saviour himself. What is needed is that sovereign work of God. What is not needed is to caste off preaching and teaching and the bringing in of more people-friendly activities and culture-friendly appropriate 'talks'. In that passage in Luke chapter 24 it says that Jesus "opened their understanding that they might understand the scriptures." This understanding and really knowing Jesus is the mighty work of God himself. We see this again spoken of by Paul in 1 Corinthians chapter 2:14 "the natural man receiveth not the things of the Spirit of God for they are foolishness unto him: neither can he know them because they are spiritually discerned." The natural man, that is to say the unbeliever cannot know nor see the things of God, it is simply impossible, there has to be this work of the Spirit. From verse 9 of the same chapter "...it is written, eye hath not seen, nor ear heard, neither have entered into the heart of man, the things that God hath prepared for them that love him. But God hath revealed them unto us by his Spirit.....We have received...the spirit which is of God, that we might know the things freely given to us of God." (verse 9,10,12). Therefore, when the word is "rightly divided" by men who are called of God, and when the Spirit is at work opening hearts and minds and ears, then Jesus is seen in all his saving glory and beauty, and God's people are mightily blessed, encouraged and strengthened.

Final Thoughts

Let me just finish and conclude this section by drawing your attention to the book of 1 Corinthians and if you could possibly read from verse 18 of chapter 1 to the end of chapter 2. Here we have a very powerful defence of the means of preaching as God's prescribed way of saving the lost and building up the saved. Paul is writing and speaking to a cultured church and yet a very carnal church; Paul is also writing to correct some of the bad practices and some of the false ideas which they had imbibed. And right here at the beginning he lays down a fundamental foundational stone in the building of God's house i.e. the preaching and the teaching of the Word of God. Here is the starting point not reasoning, philosophy, man's wisdom or debate. None of these things he uses to seek to 'correct them' or 'draw people in', or to 'befriend' them, or to 'win them over'. The Jews sought the miraculous and supernatural, "a sign". The gentiles sought academia and "wisdom" which only they could understand. (ch1:22). But Paul "preaches Christ and him crucified" and declares with a clarity that cannot be denied that "it has pleased God through the foolishness of preaching to save them that believe." (ch1:21). This, and only this has he chosen to confound the wisdom of this world, the proud, the cultured, the technologically advanced, the so-called 'intelligent and cultured ones' of our society. It is the preaching of God's holy and powerful Word by men saved, humbled and called under the mighty hand of God. "It was to be in the demonstration and the power of the Holy Spirit" and not with "enticing words of man's wisdom". (ch2:4).

We just don't like the simplicity of these words and we begin to reason "the young people wont listen; the broken family wont understand; people will just mock us, walk by and think we are being aggressive and judgemental". These are all lies from the devil because simply God has promised that he will save, he will call and he will keep his people by and through the preaching of Christ in the whole counsel of God, and it is the work of the Holy Spirit who does all the convincing and drawing and saving not our use of clever gimmicks, entertainment and numerous other people friendly activities, some of which do indeed have their place.

The apostle Paul exhorts those Roman Christians "whosoever shall call upon the name of the Lord shall be saved." (Romans 10:13) He then goes on to speak of God's prescribed way. "How shall they call upon him whom they have not believed? How shall they believe in him whom they have not heard? And how shall they hear without a preacher? And how shall they preach unless they are sent?.....So faith comes by hearing, and hearing by the Word of God". (verses 14-17, NKJV). Here we have another remarkable and definitive text. We saw in 1 Corinthians how the Holy Spirit must do his work to apply God's word, here Paul says that saving faith is actually born in the heart by hearing God's word preached. No man or woman, or boy or girl is born with the ability or the faith to believe and repent, this is given as a gift by the Lord to those who are listening and hearing the message about the crucified Christ. This is a supernatural miracle which is akin to the creation of the world. That is why one is said to be a "new creation" or to be "born again," and this experience is worked in the heart and mind as the truth is revealed to us and as we hear the message of the gospel. This experience continues as we grow in Christ in faith and as we continue with the Lord's people to hear the Word preached.

Here we have the real issues: it is God that opens the ears, the heart and raises us up from our spiritually dead condition. This he does by his Spirit through the doctrine of the Word of God, revealing a living and a risen Christ to the spiritually needy soul. The means he has chosen to use from the dawn of time to the end of history is the spoken and the written word. We must resist all thoughts of 'doing church differently' for success. No matter what the culture is, what it says or what it seeks to impose upon us, this is not from God but from the world and from the evil one. The people of God are also to be built up by the continual preaching of the Word. The church and its preaching and teaching ministry is to be enduring and permanent. Again I say, any deviation from this must be rejected completely. We must not allow the world to squeeze us into its mould but rather seek by God's grace and mighty power to change people from the world by the continual preaching and evangelising, and then to build up those in whom the Spirit calls to himself by that same preaching.

The reality is that those who are truly converted love God's truth; the Word of God is their delight; they love to hear the Word preached because just like those disciples of old their "hearts burn within them" when Jesus is revealed. Whether there are good preachers or bad preachers, it matters not, they do not 'throw the baby out with the bath water' but rather pray for those who are delivering God's message among them, and they seek to support them by their prayers and their presence in the meetings, "not forsaking the assembling of ourselves together, as the manner of some is, but exhorting one another: and so much the more as you see the day approaching." (Hebrews 10:25).

Let us begin to lay again this second very important ancient landmark and great foundational stone which has in many places been removed by hypocrites, unbelievers and 'evangelical snowflakes' alike. Let us take back the narrative and take back that which is rightfully ours and seek to reach our communities of whatever cultural background, of whatever status and build them up making them the men and women that God intended them to be.

Why We Should Believe the Entirety of the Old Testament

"For had ye believed Moses, ye would have believed me: for he wrote of me. But if ye believe not his writings, how shall ye believe my words?"
(John 5:46,47)

As we have been discussing returning to our biblical roots and laying down the ancient landmarks which have been removed by liberals and hypocrites, those liberal and unbelieving notions have certainly left their mark in the Christian church today. One particular mark is a prevailing tendency to caste doubt and dispersion upon the relevance and truthfulness of the old testament scriptures, and if we are to preach, speak and write into our times the whole gospel and the glory of a risen Christ then the old testament must never ever be caste off but rather believed entirely and completely. There is indeed widespread ignorance and misunderstanding regarding the old testament and how it applies to our new testament experience. More and more Christians regard much of the old testament as not really applicable to themselves especially those passages that they would consider the more unpalatable passages regarding wars, bloodshed and divine judgement, or those passages that tell of those miraculous and cataclysmic events like the 6 day creation, the fall of Man and the global flood etc. The modern 'snowflake evangelical' just cannot seem to square the circle between old testament Biblical History and science, or old testament Biblical History and the love, grace and mercy of Jesus. In fact in my own discussions quite often it has been said "all that matters is Jesus," or "that's just the old testament, we are living in an age of grace now," or further still "you don't really need to believe that to be saved, and we have to understand that in it's cultural context." These are actual quotations from people that call themselves Born-again Christians, and yet clearly deny the relevance of the old testament for themselves or for society in general. They have obviously swerved around the text that heads this chapter! But let us continue.

So, with these thoughts in mind I would like to explain why the old testament matters, why it is relevant, why it must be believed and accepted, and why it is entirely reliable, and why still it must be thundered from every pulpit in the land once again. To begin with I have four encouragements for us to receive God's Word as it is delivered to us in the old testament.

Firstly then:

The Scriptures Testify of Themselves
In 2 Timothy 3:16 it simply states that "all scripture is given by inspiration of God." Simple, powerful and unavoidable truth. This cannot be interpreted in any other way, it is a statement of fact and we 21st century Christians are left with a choice: to believe or to reject. All scripture is inspired of God, and all scripture comes from God himself. This is a unique and a miraculous explanation of what the bible testifies of itself. Again, we read in 2 Peter 1:16,20,21 "for we have not followed cunningly devised fables...no prophesy of scripture is of any private interpretation. For prophecy came not in old time by the will of man: but holy men of God spake as they were moved by the Holy Ghost." This word prophecy speaks of the Hebrew scriptures, the revelation of God to his people, the Jews. Individuals didn't invent these stories in the old days and pass them on, they were not "cunningly devised fables" rather they were truths that men who were "moved by the Holy Spirit" to record and recount actual, historical events of God dealing with a people and the surrounding nations. These things we are told elsewhere "were written afore time...for our learning, that we through patience and comfort of the scriptures might have hope." (Romans 15:4). All the above

texts are quotations from the new testament so we might ask of what scriptures are they telling us are all inspired by God? Well obviously they are speaking of the old testament because the new testament was still being written, it hadn't been completed yet! Those writers were looking back and as they wrote they wrote words which were verifying and testifying of the old testament that they were from God, inspired, relevant, helpful, needful and true. Another new testament writer declares of the old testament that "the Word of God is quick and powerful, and sharper than any two edged sword, piercing even to the dividing asunder of soul and spirit...a discerner of the thoughts and intents of the heart." (Hebrews 4:12). Only a divinely inspired work of God himself could do this. In Psalm 19:7-8 we read "the law of the Lord is perfect, converting the soul, the testimony of the Lord is sure, making wise the simple. The statutes of the Lord are right, rejoicing the heart, the commandment of the Lord is pure, enlightening the eyes." These words: law, testimony, statutes, commandments are all words that denote the scriptures in their entirety: The Word of God as it was being revealed in the old testament most surely testifies of itself as does the testimony of those new testament writers.

Secondly, we should believe the old testament in it's entirety because:

The Early Church Believed Them
Imagine yourself for a moment as Christians belonging to the early church. Imagine you are there while the church was in it's primitive and transitional state and ask yourself what are you to believe? How do you know it's true? How can I be sure that what these so-called apostles are teaching is true? Amidst all these monumental changes how can I be sure that this is all from God and I am not being embroiled in some Jewish/Gentile cult? Well friends, again the simple answer is the old testament scriptures. This is what the early church had

in their hands to verify what was being taught, and this was their ultimate final authority. We see this most clearly exemplified in Acts 17:11. Again, I ask you to imagine the scene. The mighty apostle Paul is preaching, that prince of the apostles declaring in demonstration of the Holy Spirit that Jesus is Lord and Saviour, that he was the promised Messiah etc., and on hearing these words the Bereans we are told "...that they received the word of God with all readiness of mind and searched the scriptures daily, whether those things were so." What scriptures were they "searching daily?" The old testament scriptures of course. Even when they heard the apostle Paul preach it had to be tested and verified against what had already been written. Paul wasn't preaching some new doctrine. Nothing he was saying would contradict what had gone before, it was only new revelational truth that would compliment Moses, the Prophets and the Law. And these Bereans studied and meditated daily, testing and checking truth against truth. These were not academics or theologians but ordinary folk just like you and me applying themselves to the study of the old testament. They had no doubts or questions regarding the veracity and truthfulness of those scriptures, but rather they went to them for the confirming of their new found Faith. Here they could see that Jesus was who he said he was; that he was the Son of God who fulfilled all those promises and prophecies, and that this was the one who would live, die and rise again to set them free from the works of the Law, justifying them and empowering them by his promised Holy Spirit to live lives of obedience unto him. It was all there in the old testament and those scriptures testify of themselves; the early church fully believed them.

Thirdly, we can be confident in the old testament because:

The Apostles Believed Them
This might seem an obvious point but as the apostles were writing the new testament those writings are replete with old

testament quotations. Every single chapter, book and page has reference to or a direct quotation from the old testament. Like I said, this was no new doctrine or new ideas; this wasn't a new religion as is often mistakenly taught. The apostles saw themselves called of God and taught by Jesus himself to build upon what had previously been written. They were being inspired and moved by the Holy Ghost to add to the divine revelation already given to his people, but this wasn't anything different only a fuller and greater revelation and insight into the mighty workings of an Almighty God. To those early church Ephesians the apostle Paul says that they were "no more strangers and foreigners, but fellow citizens with the saints, and of the household of God; and are built upon the foundation of the apostles and prophets, Jesus Christ himself being the chief corner stone." (Ephesians 2:19,20). The apostles believed and taught from the old testament and in doing so they were building upon the foundations already laid by the prophets. Again, I add that nothing was doubted, denied or even up for debate, it was all completely believed and accepted as the word of God and as such they taught the people building upon that foundation, Jesus Christ as the chief corner stone.

Fourthly, we are to believe the old testament because:

The Lord Jesus Himself Believed and Taught From Them

Again, this might seem an obvious point but given the prevailing ignorance and doubting of the old testament it appears not. In the gospels we find hundreds if not thousands of references and quotations from the old testament. Jesus speaks from them as authoritatively and even as a matter-of-fact. At the age of 12 he was found discussing with the teachers of the day in the temple; at the commencement of his ministry in Luke chapter 4 he was in the synagogue opening up, reading and preaching from the old testament book of Isaiah "as was his custom"; and throughout his brief ministry he spoke of Adam and Eve, Abraham, Sodom and Gomorrah; he made mention of Moses, Daniel, Jonah, David and Solomon; he speaks further of Noah, the Flood and of the destruction of the temple; and in all these things "beginning at Moses and all the prophets, he expounded unto them in all the scriptures the things concerning himself." (Luke 24:27). Jesus believed and taught from the old testament.

By way of application then I must ask that if the bible testifies of itself, if the early church believed the old testament, and if the apostles and Jesus our saviour believed, quoted and preached from them how dare we even contemplate for one moment doubting them or try to reinterpret them in our own "cultural context"? These issues are not up for debate! The text that heads this chapter declares simply that it really isn't possible to reject and not believe what Moses wrote i.e. about the creation, the fall, the global flood and the Ark, about the judgements of God upon Sodom and Gomorrah, it is impossible to not believe these things and yet believe the words of Jesus. They are one and the same; they are from the same source. Jesus is "The Word of God." (John 1:1; Revelation 19:13). To reject the old testament teachings is to reject Jesus himself. Let us not deceive ourselves that this isn't the case, our Lord said it himself that if we refuse to believe and accept Moses and all that he taught then how can we possibly believe Jesus and all that he teaches? It simply cannot be done. Any person who teaches otherwise is completely deluded, he is like those Pharisees whom Jesus said were like the "blind leaders of the blind."

Christians historically, have always held a high view of the whole of God's Word, nowadays however there is a pick-and-choose mentality and a rather weak and casual approach to the Bible. The ancient landmark of the old testament scriptures have, in many churches, been removed from the equation and what is left is half a gospel and a partial view of Jesus himself. We have seen in this little study four very basic encouragements for us to fully embrace the whole of the old testament, but how are they actually relevant for the new testament church? Do they really matter that much? Before I lay out my answers to those questions let me say firstly, this whole wordage of 'old' and 'new' in our day is not helpful, especially in Christian circles. It seems to imply a kind of less relevant and more relevant, that was old, in the past, it's outdated, it's not necessary or as needful, it's just the old testament; but now we have the new and the most necessary, "it's all about Jesus." This has come about because the pastors in our churches have portrayed a negative mindset upon the old testament and have failed to teach the scriptures as one whole divine revelation. As I said in a previous study about the word "doctrine," many have attached negative connotations to that word and when we hear these negative ideas week after week then consequently the people reject "doctrine" or "teaching" either subconsciously or all together. But let us continue.

The Old Testament is a:

Foundational & Unfolding Revelation
Psalm 11:3 declares "If the foundations be destroyed, what can the righteous do?" Throughout this whole little book we have been discussing foundations, ancient landmarks and boundary stones, laying down once again important biblical principles, going back to basics etc. Brothers and sisters in Christ, the old testament is one giant foundational stone, or I should say it contains a whole host of fundamental rocks upon which we must build. If those rocks are removed, if those foundations are destroyed, what indeed can the righteous do? The whole edifice will begin to crumble leaving behind fragments of truth. The new testament teaching of the apostles and of Jesus himself are built on top of what has gone

before and what God has revealed throughout the previous millennia. Every single teaching regarding Christ and all of his offices, the church and how it is to operate, how we ought to live, our relationship with the Lord, with each other and with the world cannot be understood properly and fully by new testament study alone, it is simply impossible. The scriptures are a connected whole, they are one supreme, divine, majestic revelation; but this revelation does not begin at Matthew chapter 1, it begins rather at Genesis chapter 1 and continues through to the Book of the Revelation chapter 22.

The unfolding nature of the old testament in its revelation about who God is, is wonderful as it is foundational. The true character of the Almighty Jehovah as he reveals himself gradually through the word is a powerful foundation stone in itself. All true saving knowledge begins with a knowledge of God. Not only is he the creator, but he is the supreme architect and artist within the creation. The stamp of his nature is everywhere to be seen, in all that can be heard, in everything that can be felt, in all things we can smell and everything we choose to taste. All of our senses enter into the divine attributes "for the invisible things of him from the creation of the world are clearly seen, being understood by the things that are made, even his eternal power and Godhead..." (Romans 1:20). "The heavens declare the glory of God; and the firmament showeth his handiwork. Day unto day uttereth speech, night unto night showeth knowledge. There is no speech or language where their voice is not heard..." (Psalm 19:1-3). Creation reveals that God is creative, he is kind, he is just, he is beyond complexity and yet bows to simplicity. This knowledge goes out to all flesh and is clearly understood by all for God reveals it to them, none are exempt from this knowledge. This line is followed throughout the entire old testament, revealing how great God is in his creation, how it is all subject to him. There not a storm and he has not started it; there is not a whirlwind that has not come from him; there is not an earthquake or a volcano that God has not had a hand in for not only has he made it he orders it all. Job chapters 38 & 39 speak of a God who is sovereignly and intrinsically involved in the events of the earth. The earth is not spinning on an axis of chaos but wholly controlled by God himself. He has placed the earth, the moon and the sun in their equidistant positions; he has formed the cyclical beauties of our galaxy and universe with all of the planets and stars, and he knows the number of them and "he calleth them all by their names." (Psalm 147:4). This is who God is as our creator.

Not only is he directly ordering all of his created universe but even everyone and everything in it. He raises the army and castes down the empire; he raises the kings and humbles the kings; he brings the locust and the famine, and the cold and the heat are at his will and no one else. The earth warms at his pleasure and cools at his will; and of course by his hand the pandemics strike the globe. The old testament reveals all of these truths about our God; and perhaps now some might realise why the old testament is not very popular because the world, the liberal pastors and evangelical snowflakes alike cannot cope with a sovereign God. It simply jars completely with their world-view. We are not in control of our own destiny the Lord is; but just how our choices and decisions work in all this many can argue about, suffice it to say that "our prayers and choices are interwoven into the fabric of God's design." (Al Martin, American Baptist Pastor). He is the sovereign architect and we must humbly bow the knee and acknowledge "Jesus is LORD."

We have been mainly speaking of God as creator and sovereign Lord of his world, and as we follow the thread through the old testament this informs us of who we are dealing with exactly, and when we come to John chapter 1:3 speaking of Jesus it says "All things were made by him, and without him was not anything made that was made," and again speaking of Jesus we are told in Colossians 1:16-17 "for by him were all things created that are in heaven, that are in earth, visible and invisible, whether they be thrones, or dominions, or principalities, or powers: all things were created by him and for him: And he is before all things, and by him all things consist." (Incidentally the New NIV Translation removes the phrase "by him" in both these scriptures and changes it to "in him" and "through him" thus weakening the teaching as Jesus as actual creator!) But let us continue. The point here is that those who declare "it's all about Jesus, the old testament is harsh and cruel, we live in an age of grace and choice now," I am afraid these folk are sadly deluded. "I and my Father are one" says Christ. (John 10:30) We are not dealing with two different God's; two different teachings or two different gospels; it is "one Lord and One Faith., one Baptism. One God and Father of all..." (Ephesians 4:5,6). "There is non other God but one...there is but one God the Father, of whom are all things...and one Lord Jesus Christ, by whom are all things." (1 Corinthians 8:4-6). It is this unfolding knowledge of the creator God revealed throughout the old testament that is a fundamental foundational stone to what we are told about Jesus in the new testament. This informs us of divinity, of deity, of Godhead.

When we realise that Jesus truly is God manifest in the flesh then we further realise that the God of the old testament and all his words and actions are one and the same. When God said let there be light, it was Jesus who spoke those words for he is the word; when the watery deluge drowned the wicked, he it was who commanded the rain to pour forth from the heavens; when Sodom was burned up it was by the will of Jesus for he is one with the Father; when the Red Sea parted he was there and he also wandered in the wilderness with his people; he was in the fiery pillar and in the cloud; he embodied all the workings of the tabernacle, the priesthood, the sacrifices and the ark of the covenant. He thundered from

Sinai; he was the water from the rock and he was "the captain of the host of the Lord." (Joshua 5:14) that went before Joshua to slay the inhabitants of the land. He slew Goliath of Gad and the hosts of the Philistines and he was grieved at the perpetual apostasy of the nation of Israel whom he had formed. He sent his prophets to warn them time and time again, and he raised up the Babylonians to take them away captive. He appeared in the fiery furnace and revealed future mysteries to Daniel the beloved of God. The walls of Jerusalem and the Temple were built once again by his providence and he remained with his people until the "fullness of the times had come," until God the Son should become flesh and become The Son of God. It was all leading up to this momentous event, the foundational and unfolding revelation of the old testament reveals all of this beautiful, wonderful and glorious historical reality and prophetical fulfilment.

Which leads us onto our next point on why the old testament is relevant; why are they to be believed and why they can be trusted as reliable and authoritative; and why also we reject them at our peril.

Prophetical Accuracy & Historical Reality
Jesus declared to two weary and discouraged souls (as we saw in an earlier study) "O fools and slow of heart to believe all that the prophets have spoken: Ought not Christ to have suffered these things, and to enter into his glory?" And beginning at Moses and all the prophets he expounded unto them in all the scriptures the things concerning himself," and again he says "these are the words which I spoke unto you, that all things must be fulfilled, which were written in the Law of Moses, and in the prophets, and in the Psalms, concerning me." (Luke 24:25-27,44). Remember these are the words of the Son of God himself not some ranter with his own message. It is the Christ of God that speaks and to even suggest slightly that the old testament is meaningless or of less relevance to

today's church is, I believe, blasphemy especially coming from the lips of church leaders, pastors and vicars. Others might speak from ignorance and perhaps know no better being taught by these hypocrites and false shepherds in the church. Whatever the case, many are guilty of removing the ancient landmarks and shall no doubt be held to account. As I said, Jesus is here speaking of Moses, the Law, the prophets and the Psalms, he is saying that it is all speaking clearly of the coming Messiah, of his death and resurrection, and indeed he calls them "fools" for being "slow of heart to believe" them. These prophecies concerning the coming one and his works are foundational stones that the apostles were to build upon, they are also great proofs to the reliability of the scriptures that they are indeed the word of the living God. They speak not only of Christ but of all of the nations around the middle east, of empires rising and falling, of battles, of the restoration of Israel and the rebuilding of the walls and the temple. It was all for told before time and most assuredly came to pass with nothing failing.

All this is intrinsically linked to the very historical reality concerning the scriptures. Time and time again the sands of the middle eastern regions unearth the actual towns and cities that the bible speaks of; time and again archaeology confirms the lives of all the ancient patriarchs. Abraham travelled from Ur of the Chaldees, to Haran and then onto the plains of Canaan, friends it's all there; where Isaac and Jacob sojourned, it's all there. The kings and their armies and all their battles with one another, it's all there, unearthed after thousands of years. The Hittites, the Sodomites, the Philistines; Edom, Egypt, Babylon and Syria, it's all there and much of which even remains to this day. From Jerusalem to Jericho, from Dan to Beersheba the historical reality has never been proved wrong. Indeed the archaeologists themselves often turn to the old testament scriptures for direct guidance to an area of interest, and this goes on to this very day.

But if the old testament is historically and prophetically reliable they also speak with:

Empathy and Honesty
"Whatsoever things were written aforetime were written for our learning, that we through patience and comfort of the scriptures might have hope." (Romans 15:4). If ever there was a book that has provided the deepest comfort in the deepest needs of mankind it is the bible, and especially the old testament scriptures, and the apostle Paul in this verse is saying just that. All those things written "aforetime" or in the past, in those old testament scriptures, they were written and passed down for our learning, for our instruction and our encouragement. The reason he gives: that "we might have hope" and that we might find "comfort." Again to those who regard the old testament as not of much use to modern culture and modern man they are tragically deluded and terribly misinformed; and any who teach their congregations as much take out of their hands a divine remedy of such encouragement and blessing that is unsurpassed in all the writings of mankind. If we are made in the image of our creator (and we are) then he who has spoken has spoken directly to all of our intimate humanity in the most useful and compassionate ways possible. He knows the best and he speaks the wisest to our needy condition. These scriptures are not empty, dry, dead, meaningless, religious platitudes but they are warm, loving and empathic; they are encouraging, and they altogether identify with us in all our pain, suffering and failings. This teaching comes to us because the old testament is also as honest as the day is long. God does not shy away from 'telling us how it is.' How it deals with the everyday family issues in the lives of the Israelites is truly remarkable. There is not an issue that is not dealt with and not a problem that is not relevant for today's struggling families and burdened individuals, and as has already been

mentioned these scriptures were written for that very purpose to instruct, to teach and to comfort.

As the pastor works his way through the old testament we absolutely see ourselves. We took the fruit from the tree; we struck the rock in anger; we deceived, we lied and we cheated. Those idols were our idols and those sins were our sins. We see our families in those ancient Hebrew families, with the exact same domestic issues and we see something of ourselves in the myriad individual character studies from Adam and Eve through Abraham, Sarah, Isaac, Jacob and Rebekah to Moses, Joshua, David, Solomon and Daniel. There is powerful and personal meaning and application in every verse, chapter and book, in every event, story and situation. God is speaking and God is breathing saving faith into the soul, and God is, if we would but open the old testament, drawing us unto himself declaring this is your God. These are living words from a living God, exhorting, encouraging, comforting and saving. He warns us because he cares; he rebukes us and he chastises us because he loves. The instruction and the wisdom afforded to those who do not reject the old testament is beyond comprehension. If we absorb and embrace the truths therein we shall not be deceived and deluded nor carried away with every wind of doctrine from false prophets.

Not only do we see ourselves in all those faults and failures but we see clearly a God who forgives, who offers mercy upon repentance and faith. The Lord restores his people. Adam and Eve might well have been caste out of the garden of Eden but they were not caste into hell fire. Noah found grace in the eyes of the Lord as did Abraham and the rest of the Patriarchs. Moses wasn't left to the deceptions and idolatry of ancient Egypt but God stirred up his heart and called out to him upon the Mount of God. Samson though he fell asleep in the prostitutes lap and was judged by God his hair began to grow again and with it his consecration to his God. David wasn't left to wallow in his desperate departure from God and neither was his son Solomon, both men were forgiven, restored and drawn back to the Lord. We could go on and on, but have not the time nor the space, thousands of books have already been written upon the old testament scriptures, I simply offer an overview to a specific end. The point I wish to make is that anybody who would dare to suggest that the old testament is "just the old testament, out dated, not applicable to today's culture and not relevant to modern church situations" is a stone-cold liar, deluded by Satan the arch enemy of all that is pure, good, holy and just. The truth is that you could not have a more relevant and more up to date revelation for mankind and for the church. What we have in these scriptures, I trust that we can now see, is mighty, divine, God-breathed, reliable, authoritative, inspired and meaningful truth. What we have here is one ancient landmark and boundary stone after another, one giant foundational stone after another and one indisputable truth after another all leading towards the word of God personified in Christ himself, the Messiah to the world. Without the old testament there is nothing for Christ to be built upon; his life, death and resurrection have not their full and proper meaning, it is but half a gospel, "these are they which testify of me," he says, and Paul affirms this truth by stating that "Christ died for our sins according to the scriptures; was buried, and rose again the third day, according to the scriptures." (1 Corinthians 15:3,4). What scriptures does Paul speak of? Well, there were only one set of scriptures: The Old Testament.

It is the pressures from the post-truth world that causes us to doubt the veracity of the divine record; it is the claims of the scientist, the verbal posturings of the philosophers. It is the hypocritical and unbelieving musings of the liberal theologians and the atheistic ramblings of the secular humanist that seek to intimidate bible believing Christians from our God-given calling to "preach the word." We have nothing whatsoever to be ashamed of or embarrassed about what we believe or what is taught in our bibles. It has stood the test of time through every possible prevailing culture and persecution. "Did not our hearts burn within us when he spoke to us by the way, and while he opened to us the scriptures" (Luke 24:32). Again I ask, what scriptures were these? The Old Testament! Embrace them, believe them and preach them, doubting nothing with hearts burning.

A Warning: Handle God's Word Faithfully

"To one we are the savour of death unto death; and to the other the savour of life unto life. And who is sufficient for these things? For we are not as many who corrupt the word of God: but as of sincerity...speak we in Christ."
(2 Corinthians 2:16,17)

"Therefore since we have received this ministry, as we have received mercy we do not lose heart. But have renounced the hidden things of shame, not walking in craftiness nor handling the word of God deceitfully..."
(2 Corinthians 4:1,2)

Having sought to establish the important and high place that God's word should have in our lives, churches and ministries; having sought to encourage the church that the preaching of that word should continue until this earth is no more, and having also sought to establish the importance and veracity of the Old Testament scriptures now I would warn all and any who are to take up the scriptures in their hands to deal fairly, faithfully and honestly with the word's of Almighty God. James 3:1 declares "be not many masters (teachers) knowing that we shall receive the greater condemnation." James says don't lust after this position of teacher, beware because God will require more from your hands; if you have been given much, much will be required. Paul also in the above quoted scriptures says that he did not corrupt the word of God when he spoke, nor did he handle the word of God deceitfully but taught sincerely, honestly and faithfully. He gave the due honour to the one who's ambassador he was, he represented the King of Kings and he felt the great responsibility which he had. He did not preach himself but Christ and him crucified. This wasn't his message or his philosophy; this wasn't some new religion with himself as it's spiritual guru, Oh no, this was

God's message and it was Jesus' gospel, the truth for all mankind for all ages. To the Ephesian church when he was leaving he also said "I have not shunned to declare unto you all the counsel of God" and then he warns them "for I know this, that after my departing shall grievous wolves enter in among you, not sparing the flock. Also of your own selves shall men arise, speaking perverse things, to draw away disciples after them." (Ephesians 20:27-30). Paul declared faithfully the whole truth, the whole counsel but others would come from even their own congregation, he calls them "wolves" speaking "perverse" and twisted things, handling God's word deceitfully. With tears he warns his beloved Ephesians.

Of all the callings that people can have upon the earth preaching and teaching God's word is the highest, the most noble and yet carries with it the greatest warnings and censure when the office and calling is done with corruption and deceit. In my opinion many pastors and church leaders simply do not feel the weight nor the conviction in their calling; they feel nothing of the gravitas of leading and faithfully building up the flock of Jesus and being the mouthpiece on behalf of God. There is a prevailing carnal and casual approach to the scriptures completely avoiding whole chapters, books and subjects for reasons of not wanting to cause offence or appear to judge. Whether they are actually truly saved at all is another question which I will look at later. Whatever the case the encouragement for now, to all who would take up the scriptures is to deal faithfully and to not shy away from declaring the whole counsel of God. But what must we guard against and how can we ensure that we are not of those that "corrupt the word of God?"

Adding or Subtracting?
In handling God's word deceitfully we do one of two things, we either add to God's revelation or we take away from the revealed truth. I believe that in doing any of these two things it

would encapsulate all of the twisting, the polluting, the corrupting and the adulterating that exists. All of the false teachings, heresy and blasphemy can be summed up by adding to or taking away from what the Lord has spoken and revealed, and this sin is not committed by unbelievers alone. It is very easy indeed to fall in this area. As well as hypocrites in the pulpits there are perhaps well meaning pastors and teachers that have slipped in their ministries. Perhaps human reasoning has crept in, or after many years in the ministry weariness and weakness has caused the capitulation. Perhaps the secular world and outside pressures have caused the collapse upon the battlefield. But let not the true servant of God give up or be too discouraged for there have been good men and better men that have succumbed to the world, the flesh and the devil's subtleties. The trick is to arise and fight again the Lord's battles "for a just man falleth seven times, and riseth up again." (Proverbs 24:16), and after Jonah's catastrophic departure from God the divine gracious record recounts "and the word of the Lord came unto Jonah a second time, saying arise, and go unto Nineveh, that great city, and preach unto it the preaching that I bid thee." So, all is not lost if you have fallen and failed to faithfully administer the heavenly manna, but let us continue.

I have said that it is an adding to or a taking away from the revealed truth that makes one guilty of handling God's word deceitfully, and this in turn leads to four main outcomes, though there might well be others:

God is dethrone
Self is exalted
Others are controlled
Satan is exposed as the architect.

These four things usually appear together when this sin is committed. Let us look at the case of Peter. Here we have a well meaning man, a zealous man and God's chosen man for apostolic ministry. Could such a one fall into this sin? The answer is yes when we turn to Matthew 16:14-23. Here we have the remarkable story of Jesus rebuking Peter, but before that from verse 14-20 Peter is singled out for particular praise on his declaration that Jesus was "the Christ, the Son of the living God" (verse 16). Continuing "Jesus answered and said "Blessed art thou Simon Bar-Jona: for flesh and blood hath not revealed this unto thee, but my Father which is heaven"" (verse 17). Not only does the Lord say this but goes on to change Simon's name to Peter and tell him that he shall have the keys of the kingdom of heaven and whatever he binds or loosens upon the earth shall indeed be bound or loosened in heaven. Oh, how he must have been pleased with himself, what a revelation he had received and what communications, and what a ministry he was to enjoy in the future. What Power and what prestige! No doubt he was feeling pretty puffed up with himself when Jesus began to reveal to them of his forthcoming betrayal, arrest, death and resurrection Peter burst into the conversation with his 'fresh revelation' "...he (Peter) began to rebuke him, saying "be it far from thee Lord: This shall not be unto thee." What a word from the Lord is this that even contradicted the very words of Jesus himself! Peter was adding to Jesus' words by adding his own message "This shall not be unto thee", and in saying this he was taking away from the truth already spoken from the lips of Christ.

Peter was well meaning and he was zealous and he thought he was being encouraging, but he was well off the mark and guilty of the sin of which we speak. But what does Jesus say to Peter: "but he turned and said unto Peter, "get thee behind me Satan: thou art an offense unto me: for thou savourest not the things that be of God, but those that be of man."" The words that came out of Peters mouth were a direct attack upon truth, and if we look at the four points stated above then we clearly see that the devil is the architect, though nobody else realised this, least of all Peter, "get thee behind me, Satan," says Jesus. This was also an attempt to dethrone God himself for God had spoken and this was an attempt to override the authority of Christ. Also Peter after his previous praise from Jesus sought to exalt himself by his addition of fresh revelation, and then he tried to control Jesus' actions by saying "No Jesus, this isn't going to happen to you, you are not going to be betrayed, arrested and die, what kind of words are these?" I hope we can all see how serious even well meaning attempts by believers to add to or take away from what God has already spoken, and how easily this delusion can take hold of any of us; but let us look at another situation of this.

In 1 Timothy 4:1-5 we have a warning from God, a revelation "Now the Spirit speaketh expressly, that in the latter times some shall depart from the faith..." (verse 1). I point out that this is God speaking "expressly." This is of particular note and should be of a particular interest to his hearers Paul is saying. And what we have following is an expose of those who would be adding to and taking away from the already written revelation; there would be those speaking lies, forbidding to marry people and commanding some to abstain from certain foods. (verse 3). Note how Paul says this is a "departing from the faith." (verse 1). This is rank apostasy, a falling away. As we can see we also have those four points I mentioned earlier. We see that the devil is the architect for Paul says that these teachers have been "giving heed to seducing spirits and doctrines of devils." (verse 1). False teaching, heresy, adding to or taking away from revealed truth is from the arch enemy of the church and of God "that old serpent, called the Devil and Satan, which deceiveth the whole world..." (Revelation 12:9). This is unmistakeably always the case; he is always the root cause of all tampering with the word of God, however small or great; whether it's those Wescott and Hort manuscripts as we saw earlier or through various deluded individuals both believers or unbelievers teaching things which they ought not or failing to teach things which they ought. If we understood the nature of our enemy perhaps we would take the word of God a little more seriously.

Not only is he the architect of these attempted deceptions, but the authority of God is undermined, it is "the Spirit that has expressly said..." God had spoken and his divine authority is being put into question and his revelation is being doubted. These false teachers in doing this are also trying to exalt themselves by setting themselves up as speaking new revelation on behalf of God, and again the controlling of others is their ultimate aim because in our passage they are actually trying to tell people what they can and cannot eat and who they can and cannot marry. Even in those most everyday practical issues they are seeking to teach outside the word of God and go beyond what is written and impose their own will and teachings upon them. (How many Pastors act with such a heavy hand!).

We could mention many more instances in the scriptures to show this pattern of the sin of which we speak, but let us be those that handle God's word without corruption or deceit, and let us be those who take a more serious approach to the scriptures, and have a higher view of the inspired oracles; and let us also be those who seek by God's good grace to "preach the word, in season and out of season," the whole "counsel of God" missing nothing out and adding nothing in. If we have slipped and failed in our duties then God is merciful to not condemn us or caste us off as of no use in his cause. Let us repent and pick ourselves up realising that if Peter can be recommissioned then so too can we; if Jonah can be recommissioned then so too can we, God has not finished with us yet, we might well have a specific job to do in his kingdom at "such a time as this." (Esther 4:14). But how do we, or can we differentiate between an apostle Peter situation or an apostate deceiver taken captive of the devil?

Deceived or The Deceiver?
There is a big difference between 'being deceived' and falling like Peter and actually 'being the deceiver' like those in 1 Timothy we looked at. Here we have to draw a line between the sheep and the goats, between the apostles and the apostates, between the saved and the unsaved. Like I said all can fall into this sin of not handling God's Word with the due care and attention that the Divine Oracles demand, but there is one big difference that exposes the apostate deceiver from among the true sheep and it is this: the true believer when rebuked and chastised humbles himself and returns back to the God of his salvation, whereas the unbelieving deceiver after continual rebukes hardens himself and continues in his sin refusing to heed all attempts at reason and loving correction. This is what actually reveals the true nature and condition of those who are handling the word of God deceitfully. Make no mistake about it this is a serious sin and carries with it the most serious and terrifying censures in the whole of the word of God. So, because of this it is absolutely imperative that we find out where we stand before God when we have been found adding to or taking away from the scriptures by our own ideology, or we have been exposed as having removed ancient boundary stones that God has commanded "remove them not".

What we are speaking of here is heresy, of holding heretical views, non biblical, Anti-christ notions, of thinking that we know better than God and teaching the dear people of God what we think is best and not from the scriptures alone. Isaiah 8:20 tells us plainly "to the law and to the testimony: If they speak not according to this word, it is because there is no light in them." Here we have *the* defining point. To continue in this sin; to continue speaking heresy and not teach truths which are long established biblical realities then "it is because they have no light in them." They are apostate, they are liars, they are deceivers, they are false prophets and they are not saved.

"There is no light in them", "wolves in sheep's clothing". Paul commands the church in Titus 3:10 "A man that is a heretic, after the first and second admonition, reject." True children of God on the first admonition will return and repent, but the unrepentant unbelieving deceivers will refuse to bend the knee. Paul says of such people reject them, excommunicate them and cast them out of the church and assembly of God's people. He knows that "a little leaven will leaven the whole lump" therefore it must be dealt with swiftly and decisively, no room for procrastination and indecision, this will prove fatal, the false doctrine will spread like a loathsome disease shipwrecking many a precious soul.

Paul speaks again of a situation that he had to deal with himself regarding heretical doctrine being spread among the church. In 1 Timothy 1:19,20 Paul is exhorting Timothy to hold onto to the Faith and a good conscience "which some having put away concerning the faith have made shipwreck. Of whom is Hymenaeus and Alexander, whom I have delivered unto Satan, that they may learn not to blaspheme." Paul speaking again of Hymenaeus in 2 Timothy 2:17,18 he says that he was teaching that the resurrection of Jesus was already past, that he had erred concerning the truth and that he had overthrown the faith of some. These men were not differing on the finer points of church government or the mode of baptism, No, they were guilty of teaching heresy and of erring from the truth, from those foundational stones upon which the church is built. He names Hymenaeus, Philitus and Alexander as the guilty parties, he rebukes them and he excommunicates them because they refused to listen and repent. He is warning the church of these heretics and ravenous wolves because they had "overthrown the faith of some". As I said this is a serious sin which is to be dealt with quickly and not left to fester and influence others away from Christ and the true doctrine of God.

To further emphasise the serious nature of what we speak there are two very similar and equally powerful passages that show us how serious this sin is. In 2 Peter chapter 2 and the epistle of Jude we see how God views the false prophet and the false teacher. In verse 1 of 2 Peter chapter 2 he says "but there were false prophets also among the people, even as there also will be false teachers among you, who privily (privately/subtlety) shall bring in damnable heresies, even denying the Lord that bought them..." And Jude declares to his hearers "...earnestly contend for the faith which was once delivered to the saints. For certain men crept in unawares...denying the only Lord God and our Lord Jesus Christ." (Jude 3,4). Here it is very clear what false doctrine actually is, it is denying the only Lord God and it is denying Jesus; these are "damnable heresies". Hymenaeus, Philitus and Alexander were guilty of this in saying that the resurrection of Jesus had passed. Those in 1 Timothy 4:1-5 were guilty of this in trying to impose a new diet upon their hearers and trying to impose upon them a celibate lifestyle; those in Galatia were guilty of this in trying to force their hearers to be circumcised, Paul says they were preaching another gospel and because they refused to stop judges them accursed from Christ. It is important to note that to deny Christ and be guilty of heresy and be condemned of God is not just about denying the trinity or that Christ even existed, no, rather it is clearly about the whole counsel of God as the above situations show us. You might think that whether you are circumcised or not is of no consequence, or if somebody is telling you to eat or to not eat certain foods, or who to marry doesn't really matter, but according to the bible and the apostolic writers it does.

Brothers and sisters in Christ this is all denying God and denying Jesus; this is all removing those ancient landmarks and foundational truths of the Gospel of Christ. Those who imbibe secular culture, secular ideology, modern science and liberal theology; those who deny the 6 literal day creation, the global flood, the overthrow of Sodom and Gomorrah; those who caste doubt upon the Messianic nature and Divine nature of Christ; those who blaspheme the cross-work of Jesus by stating that the Father in judging his own Son was like some type of child abuse; those who deny the resurrection, and those who deny that Jesus is the only name under heaven given whereby we must be saved. Those also who completely reject biblical morality and sexuality, and biblical truths regarding marriage, manhood, womanhood, the family and the order of authority in the home as well as that of the church; those who deny a personal devil and his influence upon the world claiming he is somehow chained and powerless, and that he must not even be mentioned in some circles for fear of "discouraging" the poor snowflake evangelicals. And those who reject almost all of the Old Testament as meaningless and irrelevant. Indeed those who continually reject and remove ancient boundary stones and fundamental tenets of the Christian Faith "once delivered to the saints" by adding to or taking away from the scriptures, such people are guilty of heresy and must be rebuked as such. Paul declares that such people's "mouths must be stopped." (Titus 1:11). This is no light matter. To reiterate we are not talking about differing views on End Time Chronology or the deeper points of the Tabernacle, I am speaking about whole swathes of fundamental, foundational truth, ancient boundaries set down for a clear demarcation of what we actually believe, who we are, what we are and what exactly is biblical Christianity!

Deeper and Wider

To many in the modern Christian church (and I have personally spoken to pastors who hold this view) just to accept the trinity and deity of Jesus is enough for acceptance and Christian fellowship. Out of such thinking has been borne the Ecumenical Movement of the World Council of Churches which is the gathering of all denominations claiming to follow Jesus in some type of unified stance to help a poor and lost world! This thinking and this movement is woefully deluded. The 'new fundamentals' for fellowship and acceptance have become increasingly narrow i.e. do you believe in Jesus? If you do then great, we can all work together! Nowadays Christians can 'agree to disagree' upon almost everything, the 'grey areas' and the 'secondary issues' have become wider and wider. More and more churches are now in full acceptance of, and will work alongside with the Roman Catholic Church just because they apparently still hold to the doctrine of the trinity, this is enough for their 'sweet unity and fellowship.' All past differences must be forgotten for the sake of 'Christian Unity and Peace.' It doesn't seem to matter about all the rank blasphemous teachings of the Catholic Church and it's total apostate practices, its idolatries and superstitions. But, hey they still believe in Jesus as Lord! Perhaps even more alarmingly some churches even accept the Muslim Cleric into their fellowship even though Islam completely rejects Christ Jesus as Messiah and Lord. In fact Islam is diametrically opposed to Christianity in every possible way. So in some circles even the deity of Christ himself is no marker of fellowship, truly does "a little leaven leaven the whole lump." This is exactly what has happened and the poor offerings of this book is a frustrated plea to open our eyes and see this wholesale capitulation and casting away of biblical Christianity.

The modern church has made the definition for unity, fellowship and acceptance a very narrow one by greatly widening the issues of non importance or issues not necessary for salvation, but they have got it completely the wrong way round. The fundamentals of the faith and necessary belief in doctrine essential for salvation is in fact much, much wider than they think. The actual 'grey areas' and 'secondary' issues are much more narrow. The whole complete word of God must be believed and accepted as true truth written by God himself, preserved down through the centuries. "It is written" declared Jesus to the devil, and to the devils of unbelievers in our day we exhort the same "it is written;" we declare with authority "thus saith the Lord." Culture is irrelevant, science is irrelevant, liberal theologians are irrelevant and snowflake Christians are also irrelevant. The scriptures with all those recorded lives, laws and statutes; with all those recorded histories and prophecies etc. recorded in the teachings of both the old and new testaments are to be believed entirely without reservation with differences of views in very, very few areas. The faith once delivered to the saints is non negotiable, it's simply not up for debate. To say "I don't believe this or that; I can't accept that, that's a bit harsh, a compassionate God wouldn't do that or say that, surely that didn't really happen like that, surely that is symbolic and metaphorical, we can only really understand that in it's cultural setting and context." To say such things or to think in such a way and approach the scriptures in this way actually is to "deny Christ," and to "reject Christ," it is to "err concerning the truth." In short it is heresy. We simply are not at liberty to pick and choose what we want to accept or reject; we cannot add to God's words or take away from the words of the Lord and begin to impose our own thoughts and ideologies upon the word. This is not an option for bible believing born-again Christians.

To become a Christian and to be saved by Jesus; to accept Christ in all his saving offices; to confess our sin and embrace Jesus as the one who lived, died and rose again for me personally is to become a new creation, old things passing away and all things becoming new. It is to accept the bible as God-breathed, God-inspired and God-written divine truth which has indeed been written for our learning, comfort and consolation with nothing to be doubted, for as James tells us plainly "...he that wavereth (doubts) is like a wave of the sea, driven with the wind and tossed. For let not that man think that he shall receive anything from the Lord. A double minded man is unstable in all his ways." (James 1:6-8). Christians can struggle with doubts and James is exhorting such to have faith and to cast off such doubts, but in our context James identifies the general characteristics of the doubters. People who are easily swayed, wandering, unstable, doubting, up and down like waves of the sea not sure what they believe or in whom they have come to believe, these folk are prime candidates to imbibe false teaching and to seek to deceive others also. Let all those who presume themselves called of God to preach be careful to not handle God's word in an unfaithful manner, or be like those who "corrupt the word of God." Be encouraged to "study to show yourself a workman approved of God," and the Lord himself will bless you abundantly in ways above and beyond you can even imagine. "To obey is better than sacrifice." (1 Samuel 15:22)

Time for a Honest, Biblical Self Examination

"Examine yourselves as to whether you are in the Faith. Prove yourselves. Do you not know yourselves that Jesus Christ is in you? - unless you are reprobate."
(2.Corinthians 13:5)

A Biblical Imperative

We have been dealing with many challenging subjects in this short little book, subjects which I personally believe are the need of the hour in which we live. I do not know in whose hands these few words might happen to fall; I know nothing of your current status or background. I am completely ignorant regarding your Christian profession or testimony; I do not know how long (if at all) you have been walking amongst the congregations of the Lord, who are as precious as the 'apple of the eye,' (Zechariah 2:8, Psalm 17:8), but one thing that I absolutely do know is that God knows! He knows and he sees all things, and all things shall have their consummation at the second advent of Christ Jesus in the last day. In that day all flesh shall stand before our great God and king, and all flesh shall be separated before him, the sheep on his right hand side and the goats on his left. Once our last breath shall leave our body there shall be no turning back, no last chances, no more opportunities, no faith to be exercised, no repentance to be done, no issues to be put right with our fellow man and no peace with God to be made. We would have either done what we ought to have done and believed upon Jesus Christ for our full, free and complete salvation, or done what we ought not to have done and rejected him outright. Given the subject matter of this book and the responsibility of those who claim to speak and live for him then is it not an absolute imperative that we ensure that we have not believed a lie, deluded ourselves and thus remain eternally ruined?

As I said we have been dealing with challenging subjects but this current study is the most challenging and the most important. I urge therefore any who read these words to not put off this necessary self inspection in the light of God's eternal Word, nor think that you might be somehow beyond such self examination. Remember the parable of the tax collector and the Pharisee as they both stood before the bar of Almighty God, one was justified who thought he wasn't and the other was lost when he thought himself saved. "The Pharisee stood and prayed thus with himself, God I thank Thee that I am not as other men are, extortioners, unjust, adulterers, or even as this publican. I fast twice in the week, I give tithes of all that I possess. And the publican (tax collector) standing afar off, would not so much as lift up his eyes unto heaven, but smote upon his breast saying, God be merciful to me, a sinner." And Jesus declared that "this man went down to his house justified rather than the other." (Luke 18:11-14). Hypocrisy in religion, self delusion and self righteousness are as common as a snow fall in the Arctic regions.

We have been discussing not removing those ancient landmarks which the Lord has put in place, those fundamentals of the Faith once delivered to the saints. We have also been looking at believing and preaching the whole counsel of God and making a zealous stand in standing for truth, righteousness and true holiness. We have sought, however weakly, to bring attention (in my opinion) to what is lacking in our churches in the western world, to strip things right back and build again from the foundations upwards a spiritual temple fit for the habitation of the triune Jehovah God. We wish to eliminate the modern 'evangelical snowflake' mentality which capitulates at the slightest confrontation and swings which ever way the cultural wind is blowing. We have sought to bring the minds, hearts and souls of the reader to a fixed position "taking every thought captive to Christ," and to his Holy, divinely inspired written Word. It naturally follows from such exhortations that persistent failure to obedience in these areas needs to be rebuked (which we have sought to do throughout the book) and serious questions asked regarding whether one is truly saved at all. Throughout the gospels Jesus is constantly bringing such self examination to bear upon the religious leaders leaders of the day, from his open rebukes, to his warnings and to all the parables he spoke directly of them, and he spoke these things not to curse them but to save them, and from a motivation of love. Our motivations in this book are the same, as were the apostle Paul's who wrote the above text to the wayward Corinthians. To all the carnal behaviour; to all the rejection of biblical authority in the apostle Paul himself; to all the toleration of sin in all it's vilest forms he simply has to ask those Corinthians to "examine themselves", "are you actually saved at all, or are you terribly deluded?" We have to ask the same questions, the same self examinations must take place. Failure in obedience to God precludes a serious and earnest questioning of our professed born-again experience, or any spiritual experience for that matter. So, let us continue.

Considering the text which heads this chapter we are most definitely on biblical ground in examining ourselves whether we are actually in the faith or not, and the questions that spring out of the above text are of the utmost importance and carry an eternal weight of significance. Our answers to such questions will determine whether we are actually on our way to heaven to be with our Lord and saviour, or on our way to a lost, endless, burning judgement. I do not ask how long you have made a profession of being a Christian; I do not ask have you been to bible college and I do not ask how many years you have been preaching or even pastoring churches. These are not very important questions at all, they mean nothing before God. I ask however, are you a real true Christian? Are you really and truly saved? Do you really know the Lord Jesus

Christ? Is your acquaintance with the things of God a genuine, saving, life-transforming born-again experience? Or have you been tragically deluded and deceived? These and other like questions must be answered if we are serious in our interest in the Lord Jesus, this cannot be emphasised too much because the deceived soul has two great enemies on this point that will help in damning the soul.

The first enemy we have is:

The Devil
Many liberal theologians will deny a personal devil, an actual person, a fallen angel, which is ironic given the fact that the bible teaches that he himself is the arch deceiver. He is spoken of throughout the scriptures as deceiving and deluding individuals, families, churches and even nations. The scriptures say he was caste out of heaven and "deceiveth the whole world." (Revelation 12:9). Not just a part of it, and not just a few persons here and there but the whole world. This is how powerful he actually is and this is how subtle and how devious. He is no fairy tale bogey man to frighten little children but rather a very real and a very powerful enemy of God and of all mankind. He will have your soul damned in hell any which way he can, and one of his chief designs is to completely deceive the soul that it is truly saved when in fact it is as hell-bound as he himself is. This deceptive nature of the devil must inform our understanding of him regarding the things of which we have been speaking and the subject of this chapter of being deluded that we are saved when in fact we are not. But how actually does he deceive and how does he trick people into believing lies and falsehoods?

In 2 Corinthians chapters 11 through 12 Paul is defending his authority and Apostleship against those who had been persuaded that Paul wasn't who he said he was. There were those among the Corinthians that were claiming to be apostles themselves and denying that Paul had received such authority and the call of God. In that 3rd verse he begins "I fear, lest by any means, as the serpent beguiled Eve through his subtlety, so your minds be corrupted from the simplicity that is in Christ." Paul makes the connection straight away "I fear, as the serpent beguiled Eve...so your mind be corrupted..." Paul recognises the devil's handiwork when he sees it. "That old serpent called the devil and Satan." (Revelation 12:9). Paul is worried and deeply concerned that his beloved Corinthians have been equally beguiled into believing lies and he fears that a great deception has taken place because they so easily accept these false teachers. He continues, verse 4 "for he that cometh preacheth another Jesus, whom we have not preached,..ye receive another spirit which ye have not received [and] another gospel which ye have not accepted." So these new 'teachers and apostles' came preaching another Jesus, another gospel in another spirit, and the Corinthians received it all as wholesome truth and divine revelation even though it was "another." It was different from what they had previously heard, it contradicted the former truth which Paul taught them through much tears. These 'apostles' came as bible teachers, evangelists, prophets and preachers and they gave themselves the pre-eminence and set themselves up as leaders in the churches, but (as we have previously studied) they were either taking away or adding to the word of God, replacing truth with their own humanistic and secular ideologies. Paul explains further who these men were in verse 13: "for such are false apostles, deceitful workers, transforming themselves into the apostles of Christ." Not only were they themselves false and deceived, but they sought to teach falsehoods and deceive others also.

Paul began by connecting these false teachers and the Corinthians to "the old serpent, the devil," and he continues exposing him who's fingerprints where all over this situation, "for Satan himself is transformed into an angel of light. Therefore, it is no great thing if his ministers also be transformed as the ministers of righteousness." (verse 14,15). And here we have the final conclusion, he hits the nail squarely on it's head, Satan is the one who has at some point appeared to these men and beguiled them with his beauty and glory, with his majesty and power, as a very "angel of light." Why is this significant to us? Well, it is significant because the devil can give very real supernatural experiences, he can illuminate the heart, the mind and the soul with extraordinary revelations. He can so move the emotions and the will by his deceptions that one can think that they are caught up to the heavens. O yes, as "an angel of light", just like before he fell into sin, old "Lucifer, son of the morning," (Isaiah 14:12) the great deceiver, this is his whole aim and object to delude and to deceive and eventually to damn the soul in a lost sinners hell. King Saul had his spiritual experiences and was lost. Judas also had his spiritual experiences, and he too was lost and these false apostles at Corinth no doubt had their experiences, and they to would be lost forever unless they repented and believed the true gospel.

Think for a moment of many of the worlds religions and cults which are usually started by some individual who testifies of heavenly visions and angelic visitations. Not only are they themselves deluded but they go on to seek to delude and deceive thousands of others. It is the devil himself who is behind all this religious delusion. O dear soul do not trust in an experience, this is not knowing Jesus and this is not salvation, beware the devils delusions on this point.

This delusion will be a particular characteristic of the last days when we are told that "the coming of the lawless one is according to the working of Satan, with all power, signs, and lying wonders, and all unrighteous deception among those that perish, because they did not receive the love of the truth, that they might be saved." (2 Thessalonians 2:9-11). Such will be the false power, deceptions and tribulations of that age that even the Lord's people will be in grave danger and those days will be cut short "for the elects sake." "False Christ's (anointed ones) and false prophets will arise showing great signs and wonders, so as to deceive if possible even the elect." (Matthew 24:21-25). We are dealing with spiritual realities here not fables and stories, and this spiritual battle is going on all the time, everyday, and every minute of the day and will have its culmination right at the very end. And one thing that characterises this battle is deception and delusion. The Bible is full of people who have fallen foul to the devils delusions and it started right at the beginning with our first parents (as we have mentioned a couple of times already). Remember what the old serpent said to Adam and Eve, "has God said you will surely die?" (Genesis 3:1,4). Has he really said that? Did he really mean that? Are you absolutely sure about that? You are not going to die." Jesus calls the devil "the Father of lies" in John 8:44. We are also dealing with "a roaring lion seeking whom he may devour." (1 Peter 5:8). Do not think that he cannot or will not try and deceive you, or even that he already hasn't, this is what this whole book is really all about. Ask yourself: am I guilty of removing the fundamental landmarks that God himself has set? Do I add to or take away from God's divine revelation? Am I ever zealous for the kingdom of Christ? Have I imposed secular ideology upon the word of God? Do I really care about having the best available translation to preach from myself or encourage the flock of Christ to read from? Is the old testament like a dead, dry document to me? Do I even believe much of what it has to say? Do I care? Am I interested? Honest answers to these questions could well ascertain the devil's delusion or Jesus' salvation and this is what the Bible exhorts all people who confess that they belong to the Lord to do: Examine themselves.

The second great enemy we have is:

The Heart
Not only do we have Satan as a subtle enemy but we have the equally subtle 'self', our own hearts as a great deceiver of the soul. God himself declares through Jeremiah the Prophet in chapter 17 verse 9 that "the heart is deceitful above all things and desperately wicked: who can know it?" Remember we are dealing with the Word of God, his record and his truth concerning all flesh. The Lord declares "deceitful above all things." If this is the Lord's testimony upon the whole mass of humankind, then ought we not take great heed to the warning especially when our eternal destiny is at stake? But how is the heart so deceitful? What does this and other like passages mean? Well, it is so desperately deceitful because the heart being the seat of the soul is so corrupted, so polluted, and so dark and devious and so full of sin that it simply cannot be trusted, and it cannot be relied upon to give a faithful record of truthful experience. Jeremiah asked the question regarding the heart "who can know it?" It is so wicked and so deceptive that it cannot be truly known, it's depths cannot be fully explored, it is full of many unfathomable and dark mysteries, intentions and motivations, but God knows and he sees, and he alone is able "to search the heart...and give every man according to his ways, and according to the fruit of his doings." (Jeremiah 17:10). Jesus himself declared that "out of the heart proceed evil thoughts, murders, adulteries, fornications, thefts, false witnesses, blasphemies." (Matthew 15:19). And Ecclesiastes chapter 9 verse 3 says that "...the heart of the sons of men is full of evil, and madness is in their heart while they live, and after that they go to the dead." Think of it, all those emotions, all those feelings, and all those desires and affections working together to totally delude, deceive and eventually damn the soul. All that untrustworthy self understanding beguiling our own selves.

We find another terrifying testimony regarding the heart of humankind in Genesis chapter 6 verse 5 where we read, "The Lord saw that the wickedness of man was great in the earth, and that every intent of the thoughts of his heart was only evil continually." What we have here is continuity. This deception, evil and wickedness doesn't stop, it continues, it goes on and on in individuals throughout their short lives and it covers the whole earth. In that word "every intent" we see that there is always some ulterior motive, some sinister design in all our thinking. We might find this hard to believe but this is God's record of the workings of the human heart, of our thought life, our emotions, will and affections. There is no other thing (apart from the devil himself) that is more evil, deceptive, corrupt, dangerous and delusional. The devil has indeed fertile soil with which to work, the seeds he casts upon the human heart and mind will grow very, very quickly and produce much poisonous and deadly fruit. It is just as easy and natural for us to indulge in every conceivable vice as it is to breathe in the air. The tragic irony in all this is that we actually really believe that we are enlightened and wise; we actually think that we are learned, that we have knowledge. Oh how foolish we are, we would do well to stop and think and consider these things, how easily we would delude our own selves. This is why we need an outside source, a genuine faithful testimony which is not partial and which has our very best interest at heart-The Scriptures. And this is also why the devil has for all of the earth's existence laboured tirelessly to undermine the Word of God and to corrupt the original text.

There are indeed many, many other verses and whole passages in the Word of God that expose mankind's true nature and we cannot just simply brush off this record of God as hyperbolic language and exaggeration to make some greater point, this is divine revelation, true truth and a faithful witness. Would we dare call God a liar!? God forbid! In accepting the objective witness of the Father, Son and Holy Spirit, in the court room of God we are found guilty. Our testimony regarding ourselves, as I said earlier, cannot be relied upon, it is not a faithful testimony, our evidence is full of holes and we have no meaningful defence at all: we are condemned. In the context of the subject of this book and of this particular chapter we have to conclude that we would deceive ourselves that all is well and we would deceive ourselves that the word of God doesn't really matter or what bibles we have in our hands, or what we actually teach the people. We would deceive ourselves that the fundamentals of the faith are of no consequence to modern mankind, and we would deceive ourselves that preaching the whole counsel of God doesn't really matter or standing zealously for the truth is not necessary. We would deceive ourselves that there will be no eternal judgement, and no hell for false teachers/preachers etc. and we would finally deceive ourselves that we are saved and that our eternal welfare is sound and secure. To any who read these exhortations consider that these devilish delusions and self deceptions are a dangerous and a most fearful reality.

We see this delusion further examined and explained whether it's from the devil or from our own hearts in the testimony and warning of Jesus himself in the 7th chapter of Matthew where we have:

The Many
Who are these many? Well, tragically these are the hundreds of thousands, if not millions of deluded souls. This is a great company, a multitude of religious people, thousands of church goers and church workers. Here we have pastors and preachers, vicars, elders and deacons; here also are perhaps evangelists and theologians, "many" individuals who are totally deluded that they are on their way to heaven. Oh dear friends, please consider these things: that it is indeed most possible and highly probable that religious deception on a vast scale is the actual experience of millions in our day. What do these "many" have to say for themselves on the day of reckoning? What is their cry of self defence before the judge of all the earth? It is this: "Lord, Lord have we not prophesied in thy name? And in thy name caste out devils? and in thy name

done many wonderful works?" (Chapter 7:22). This is their plea before him who has eyes as a flame of fire, this is their plea before the one who's name they have had often upon their lips, but this is their plea to the one who it now appears never dwelt in their hearts, for he himself declares "I never knew you, depart from me, ye that work iniquity." (verse 23). Jesus had previously warned the disciples "not everyone that saith unto me Lord, Lord shall enter the kingdom of heaven," (verse 21), and here now the fearful and awful reality hits home. Remember, we are not dealing with outright atheists in this passage, we are not dealing with people with no profession of faith whatsoever, Oh no, we are talking of church goers and workers in the church, even miracle workers in the church! We are dealing with Pastors, preachers, teachers, evangelists, theologians and bible teachers. We are talking of those who have pre eminence in the churches, religious leaders etc. These are the many and these are the thousands to whom Jesus will declare "I never knew you." Can you not hear the cries of absolute anguish and despair from all those millions of deceived souls? Now it's all too late, the time for them to examine themselves to see whether they are in the faith is past, the time to make their election and calling sure is gone forever, all that now remains is for the final, fiery indignation which burns the adversaries of the Lord Jesus to fall upon them. Oh dear, precious soul I earnestly plead with you to at the very least consider these things and not cast them off as having no relevance for yourself. Whether it's the devil or whether it is self, a great deception has been wrought here.

Being a Christian, knowing the Lord Jesus Christ and living and working for him is a hard and a narrow path, and it is those who are described in this passage as:

The Few
We now ask who are these "few?" And what are the marks of the few? It is primarily those "who do the will of their Father in heaven" (verse 21) who shall enter the kingdom of God.

This doing the will of the Father is not doing great wonders, casting out devils and prophesying, neither is it seeing visions or experiencing other spiritual and supernatural happenings. It is not in preaching, praying, or meditating, neither is it in understanding great mysteries and knowledge; it isn't in life-long church attendance, nor in walking forward in some evangelical campaign or in being baptised, or even in giving thousands to the church. It is not even in giving your body to be burned in some ultimate self sacrificial way, (there are many fanatical religious martyrs), all this will not save the soul. If all these things were to be accomplished in one man or one woman they will not bring them into favour with the One, True and Living God. This doing the will of the Father is firstly to believe, to have faith, to embrace Christ Jesus. There were those in the gospel of John who asked "What shall we do that we may work the works of God? Jesus answered and said to the them "this is the work of God that you believe in him whom he sent."" (John 6:28,29). And again we read that "Whosoever believeth that Jesus is the Christ is born of God.." (1 John 5:1). So, firstly those who do the will of the Father are those who believe in him whom he has sent. It is faith that appropriates God's salvation in and through Jesus Christ. "By grace are ye saved, through faith; and that not of yourselves: it is the gift of God, not of works lest any man should boast." (Ephesians 2:8,9) And again from Romans chapter 10:9-11,13 "If thou shalt confess with thy mouth the Lord Jesus, and shalt believe in thine heart that God has raised him from the dead, thou shalt be saved. For with the heart man believeth unto righteousness; and with the mouth confession is made unto salvation. For the scripture saith, whosoever believeth on him shall not be ashamed...For whosoever shall call upon the name of the Lord shall be saved." This "doing the will of God" from Matthew 7:21 is not meant actual good works for this would contradict the clear teaching from other passages as we have seen, "not of works lest any man should boast." Paul says also in Romans 3:20 "for by the deeds of the law (doing good works) there shall no flesh be justified in his sight..." Our perceived wisdom, works, knowledge or even spiritual experiences do not and cannot ever move the heart of God favourably towards us to save us, but rather to be in a right standing with God, that is to say justified before him or made righteous to stand before him we have to look to another to be our advocate, saviour, redeemer, righteousness and substitute, and this other is Jesus. In believing him to be all this for us we shall be saved. This is what God requires. "The righteousness without the law (not by our own good works) is manifest (or revealed) being witnessed by the law and the prophets (spoken of clearly in the old testament); even the righteousness of God which is by faith of Jesus Christ, unto all and upon all them that believe....Therefore we conclude that man is justified by faith without the deeds of the law." (Romans 3:21-22,28).

Faith, which is God's free gift is the means by or the conduit through which all of God's grace, salvation and saving love flows into our souls. It is the channel by which we receive all that God has to offer us, and through which we are born-again, made a new person and actually become a new born Christian. This faith has a definite object, that object is a person and that person is Jesus. He is the only answer and way to be saved, it is in him and in him alone that salvation exists. It is in his name alone and in his works, not ours, that our relationship with our creator and heavenly Father is to be restored. "I am the way, the truth and the life, no one cometh unto the Father but by me," says Jesus in John 14:6. When we reject hope in our selves and trust in Jesus and believe in him then we are adopted into the great company of God's people, usually called the Church Universal. We become a true son or a true daughter of God, Christ being our elder brother. What a wonderful salvation this is and what a simplicity there is in Christ to be saved. There is no room for intellect or academia, by that I do not mean that God bypasses the mind, I mean in an advanced, academic adult sense. This salvation isn't attained by gaining some sort of advanced, heightened and illuminated state of existence, it is simple, childlike faith. This is a trust and a gospel that a child can understand but a knowledge that eludes the greatest minds; these are spiritual truths about a real person that fasten themselves to the heart, the soul and the mind that brings such a saving conviction that Jesus is Saviour, Christ and Lord. (Luke 2:11).

The second thing that we do to do the will of the Father is to repent of our sins. It is to turn from, to be truly sorry for and to ask forgiveness for all of who we are and what we have thought and done. The message of John the baptist was "repent for the kingdom of heaven is at hand." (Matthew 3:2). The message of the apostles when the crowd cried out "men and brethren, what shall we do?" was "repent". (Acts 2:37,38). And again, "repent therefore and be converted, that your sins may be blotted out." (Acts 3:19). Jesus told his disciples to preach a message of "repentance and remission of sins in his name to all nations." Luke 24:46,47). So it is most clear from the Word of God that this doing the will of the Father and those few who shall be saved must first repent and believe the gospel. It is turning and believing; it is sorrowing and then following, and it is forsaking and then embracing Jesus Christ who lived a righteous life for us, who died a sinners death for us and who arose a Divine, victorious saviour for us. This is what the few do; this is the starting point; this is where a soul is said to be "born-again" and become "a new creation old things passing away, behold all things become new." (2 Corinthians 5:17).

It could be said that repentance is "a work" and therefore should not be preached for anyone to be saved, just "faith alone." Well, to that I would say that Jesus calls faith "a work" as we have seen "this is the work of God, that you believe..." (John 6:29). And it is true, anything that is an act of the will and an exercise of the emotions or affections could rightly be assumed to be a work. But, it is not the work that saves it is God. These particular attributes of the will i.e. faith and repentance are, it must be remembered: gifts of God. They are graces that are the result of the work of the Spirit, unseen by man. They are the stirrings of the soul, the moving of the affections and desires, the persuading or drawing of the will, which are the active volition of the human person. Faith is the gift of God and repentance might be said to be a quality of true faith. One cannot turn from sin towards God (repentance) without first having faith, and one cannot have faith (believe and embrace Jesus) without it being given by God himself. The truth is that we end up splitting and dissecting texts which God does not require us to do so. The facts are that God commands both: Faith and Repentance as all the scriptures above quoted testify to. Our responsibility is to obey. If the Lord says believe and trust in him then we shall; if the Lord commands repentance, turning from idols to serve the living God, then we shall. These qualities are so intimately joined together that it is absolutely impossible to separate them. That is why I said that repentance is a quality of faith. If one is to repent, what exactly is he repenting from and to? In turning from sin towards God one simply has to believe for that act to be accepted by God. We are saying that we are leaving behind a life of sin and turning towards God for salvation and committing yourself as a slave to live a holy life. Let us just obey and we shall be saved.

It is therefore these people who have truly believed and have truly repented who also have certain characteristics, and these characteristics or evidences of true faith are to be found in the epistle of 1 John. These tests or this examination of oneself is clearly set out in this epistle and it might be summed up in asking yourself several questions to ascertain whether your profession of owning and knowing the Lord Jesus is real and genuine or not. The new born Christian has three things which he loves and he has two things which he now hates.

The true Christian now loves:

The Lord
The Commandments
The Brethren

The Bible declares and our experience should concur that "we love him, because he first loved us". (1 John 4:19). Oh yes, we love God in is triune beauty and glory; we can't explain it and we don't fully understand it but we know it is true and that we cannot deny it-We Love God: Father, Son and Holy Spirit because he "first loved us." He saved us and he came to us in our waywardness, lost estate and in our filth. He came to us when we were spiritual lepers, unclean and hell-bound but Christ has come and touched us, embraced us and had compassion upon us. He has given us faith to embrace him, repentance to turn from our sin, new desires and affections to live for him and his Holy Spirit to empower us. If you know nothing of that which I speak then it can only be concluded that you are a stranger to Christ and that "ye must be born again". (John 3:7).

Again, a true Christian loves the commandments of God, and because he loves his Word he seeks with all that God-given power to obey, and so says John again "By this we know that we know him, if we keep his commandments," and again "whoever keeps his word, truly the love of God is perfected in him, by this we know that we are in him."(1 John 2:3,5). John tells us clearly and explicitly that the true Christian loves the commandments of God, and in loving them obeys them, Oh yes there will be falls and failures but this doesn't change his hearts desire. If the statutes of the Lord; if the precepts of Almighty God are a burden to you and you have no liking or longing for holiness then sadly it can only be concluded that you are not saved and need as a matter of urgency to get the real thing at the foot of the cross.

Let me go on, John also declares in that first epistle that "in this are the children of God and the children of the devil manifest: whoever does not practice righteousness is not of God, neither is he who does not love his brother," and again, "he who does not love does not know God, for God is love." (ch.3:10, ch.4:8). Dear soul to love the brethren is another clear sign that we are truly born-again and that our experience is real, true and saving. Scriptures could be multiplied from this epistle. I ask any who are unsure to go home, find a secret place, open the first epistle of John and prayerfully consider your soul. Ask yourself, do you really love the commandments, the laws, and the principles of God? Though there is weakness and sin to be confessed still is your great desire to keep the word of your Father in heaven? Do you also have that inward love for the people of God which you never had before? Are God's people the apple of your eye as they are their heavenly Father's? If you can wholeheartedly answer yes then I'm sure your faith and repentance is real, that your justification, redemption, and sanctification is not to be doubted, and that your inward apprehensions of Jesus are also genuine and saving. It is only possible to love God's laws and to love his people when we have the love of God shed abroad in our hearts, and this can only happen when we are born-again by the Spirit of God.

The Christian now has two hates, and these are:

The World
Sin

Again, carrying on in this first epistle of John "If anyone loves the world, the love of the Father is not in him,"(ch.2:15). John is so clear and plain, he just says it like it is, these truths are so simple. James agrees with these sentiments in his letter for he declares "friendship with the world is enmity against God". (James 4:4). The new born Christian hates the world and all it stands for, it's a trouble to him, it pains him and it grieves him. How so? Well, all its philosophies and ideologies, and all its greed and corruption, all its anti-Christian attitudes and blasphemies seeking to break in upon him and bring him down, seeking to influence all of his thought life and behaviour. He now sees it for what it really is; it's all a lie and a delusion and keeps the masses gripped in its leisure and pleasure, and its sin and depravity. The Christian, by the grace and power of God has escaped it and now he continues to flee from it for he hates it, this has become a matter of life and death for him. To love this world the Bible clearly tells us is to be in a state of conflict with God and the Love of God simply cannot reside in such a heart.

As it is with the world so it is with sin. Let me ask you some questions. What do you think about sin? How do you view it? When you fall does it grieve your soul? Does it upset you when you upset somebody else? Or do you have a pretty relaxed view about sin? Are you casual regarding the laws of God? Do you take a similar casual approach to the gatherings of God's people? Do you still frequent the old haunts, not really caring for all that language, blasphemy and crude conversation? Or does it truly grieve your soul? Again and again in this epistle it declares "by this we know him," "by this we know that we have passed from death to life." "by this we know we are of the truth," "by this we know that he abides in us." It is all by these simple tests and examinations. Ask yourself openly, honestly and prayerfully the questions of 1 John, and if you can answer yes once again you will find that you possess a real Faith and are not amongst those "many" who are sadly and tragically completely deluded and deceived.

Tests in Context
The heading of this particular study is exhorting us to a honest, biblical self examination; and the context for this challenging and heart searching message is Pastors, preachers, Christian leaders, elders, deacons etc. adding to or taking away from God's word in removing the ancient fundamentals of the Christian Faith, and in completely capitulating and melting away like a snowflake being easily offended and fearful of offending others. The message is to those who have no zeal, no fire, no fight and no passion for the Christian battleground, or who care not whether they have a blunted sword in their hands, or a much more superior and unalloyed Jerusalem blade (as Bunyan puts it) that "is quick , and powerful, and sharper than any two edged sword, piercing even to the dividing asunder of soul and spirit, and of the joints and marrow, and is a discerner of the thoughts and intents of the heart. Neither is there any creature that is not manifest in His sight: but all are naked and opened unto the eyes of him with whom we have to do." (Hebrews 4:12-13). The multitude of new translations and various paraphrases are a pathetic attempt at fulfilling this verse, for they are weak, insipid and powerless. The Christian pastor should be crying out "give me the double edged sword, give me the Jerusalem blade above all others, for this, and this alone will do the job that God requires: piercing, discerning, dividing, manifesting and saving souls."

If you have failed in the areas that I've mentioned in this short treatise then of necessity you must examine yourself whether you have truly embraced the Jesus of the Bible or whether you have in fact embraced one of yours or someone else's imagining. I state this because, as we have seen, the devil's delusions are strong as are your own hearts. There is nothing in the entire existence of humanity that is more deceptive and capable of deluding self than your own heart and the devil. This situation is not unusual but is very common, indeed multitudes will cry out in the last judgement, again as we have seen, "many will say to me in that day, 'Lord, Lord, have we not prophesied in thy name etc.?" and Christ declares "I never knew you, depart from me." (Matthew 7:22,23). This is a most fearful reality that simply must not be brushed aside as inconsequential.

A Word to the Deceived
If you have failed in the areas of this book then your are in one of two camps. You are either under the spell of self delusion believing that God is your God and that you know Jesus when tragically you do not, or you are also terribly deluded and fallen from your masters service but still truly saved. These are the only two options or outcomes of Pastoral/teaching/ministering/leading failure with regards to what is taught in this book and the resulting capitulation. If on self examination you find yourself totally deluded and a false minister of Christ then all is not lost, for you have chanced upon this message. Many a minister of the gospel down through the centuries found themselves unconverted whilst even doing the Lord's work, the most famous being the great German reformer Martin Luther, and off course John Wesley, the great evangelist of the The Great Evangelical Awakening. You are in good company there! But you are at a critical, pivotal moment in your history. It is time to 'carpe diem', seize this day and moment, choose this day whom you shall serve. If you have gotten this far then something has held your attention (not that of the poor writer) but God. He is calling you to himself no doubt; he is opening your eyes to true truth and spiritual reality, and the clear message to you from Paul's second epistle to the Corinthians, chapter 6:2 is "...behold now is the accepted time; behold now is the day of salvation." Delay no longer, you can stifle the conscience no more, God is pouring out his love and grace, take it, embrace it, believe it; bend the knee, repent and believe the gospel before the gospel door is bolted shut to you for ever more. Again with Paul "we

beseech you...we pray you in Christ's stead, be ye reconciled to God. For he hath made him to be sin for us, who knew no sin; that we might be made the righteousness of God in him." (2 Corinthians 5:20,21).

Be encouraged, for there is all the encouragement in the world to turn to Christ and be saved. You shall escape a hypocritical existence deceiving no one but yourself, and you shall escape the wrath that is to come, which shall come upon all who have not Christ as their saviour and Lord. Do not be too proud or too stubborn to examine yourself, it is no shame to find yourself deluded, rather it is the great grace and love of God in helping you to be un-decieved. If you are found wanting then heed the exhortation of 1 John 1:9 and along with all those who have trod the narrow way, together with them let us "confess our sins" for "he is faithful and just to forgive us, and to cleanse us from all unrighteousness." We can then freely belong to that great multitude from every tribe, nation, and tongue who shall at the last day enter into the great glory and worship him "who loved us and washed us from our sins", and delivered us from the lies and the deceptions of the devil. Hallelujah and Amen.

To all the backsliding Pastors/teachers/leaders etc., to all you who have found that your self examination has shown that your saving interest in Christ is real and true but that you have seriously caved-in from the multiple carnal, cultural pressures of the day, to you I would dare to say "humble yourselves therefore under the mighty hand of God, that he may exalt you in due time; casting all your care upon him, for he careth for you. Be sober, be vigilant for your adversary the devil, as a roaring lion, walketh about, seeking whom he may devour; whom resist, steadfast in the faith..." (1 Peter 5:6-9). Peter who wrote these words knew from painful, personal experience what failure and denial was all about, but he also knew what recommissioning and repentance was all about as well. What an example of grace and mercy he is. Do you feel weak and weary? Do you feel yourself incapable, incapacitated and unusable? Look to Peter, but in looking to Peter look to Christ the restorer of Peter. Remember "a bruised reed he shall not break, and the smoking flax he shall not quench." (Isaiah 42:3). However much of a failure you actually are or feel that you are there is always a way back to your heavenly Fathers service. Again, you have read thus far for a reason, and the reason is God is looking for men to repent, arise and stand in the gap of these last days; he is looking for men to trust in him, to be filled by his Spirit and move from cowardice and failure to boldness and victory. It happened to the apostles it can happen to you. They denied, they fled and they feared their culture, and they fell, but that was not the end, Jesus had other plans for the ones whom he had chosen for the task ahead.

Many others within the Word of God have fallen under various pressures and yet have found grace again with God, some we have already alluded to in earlier studies. Jonah is a fine example of frail flesh falling but of God recommissioning and resending. He point blank refused to obey the call of his master, he didn't want to go to Nineveh and preach to them for he knew that God would and could save them. Jonah did not want them to be saved but to perish, (as is clear when he waited and watched what would befall the city Chapter 4:5) so he fled. He was an angry man and the very reason he fled and disobeyed God in the first place he tells us after he saw God have mercy upon all the inhabitants of the city the scripture declares "but it displeased Jonah exceedingly, and he was very angry....was not this my saying when I was yet in my country? Therefore I fled....for I knew that Thou art a gracious God, and merciful, slow to anger and of great kindness." He must have been the worlds worst preacher, actually not wanting souls to be saved but to burn!! The Lord had to teach him a lesson from this blind spot of his carnal flesh. He didn't cast off

Jonah; the Lord did not set him aside and send someone else, No, Jonah must go and fulfil his ministry with God making him a wiser and more compassionate man in the process. Is this you? Has the great whale of this world swallowed you up and spat you out onto the shores uselessness? Do you literally feel 'all washed up' and even ready to die like Jonah. "Caste me into the sea" he says "take, I beseech Thee, my life from me" he prays, "it is better for me to die than to live," he foolishly declares. (Ch.2:12, 4:3,8). It is a good job that not all our prayers are answered as we would like them to be when we are in our worst moments. Our God sees the bigger picture and that includes you to take up the sword of the Spirit, God's eternal Word and Preach again the preaching that the Lord bids you preach, fearing nothing but God and sin.

A Short Interlude and Summary
The current pandemic of apostasy which infects many thousands if not millions of precious souls with a deadly, dark and devious spiritual virus has indeed been unleashed across Christendom and has been spreading for many, many years rendering the Evangelical Church incredibly diseased and weak, with no meaningful witness. In the previous chapters we have sought to 'get back to basics' as it were; we have sought to strip things right back and attempt to expose the real issues and answer the whys. We have not sought to prove for instance a literal 6 day creation from God's Word (which we could) but to ask and to answer: why Christian Pastors do not teach a literal 6 Day creation. We have not sought to prove that homosexuality is a sin, or that marriage between a man and woman is God's order but rather to ask how and why the Church has removed that ancient boundary stone. Again we have not sought to prove a whole host of biblical fundamentals but rather to reveal why the modern evangelical Christian snowflake leaders have completely capitulated in standing for truth and sought to insert into their own ministries and their own (or others) humanistic reasoning, philosophies and ideologies.

We have started right at the beginning and have sought to emulate those great leaders of both the English Reformation and the European Reformation by seeking to encourage today's preachers/leaders that it is absolutely imperative to have the finest "double edged sword" in their hands. Preaching God's word is the highest office and the highest honour afforded any individual upon the earth, among all people, from all classes and in all of the estates of life itself. And because it is no light thing to take up the "Holy Oracles of God" it naturally follows that one must have the best translation in the language which one speaks. We have sought to encourage God's people, especially the preachers to completely reject the modern ideology of the today's Bible

Colleges of trying to intellectualise Textual Criticism by imposing 'Dynamic Equivalence' upon the text. We simply have not got that authority to change any text of scripture to make it 'more easy' for the people of God to understand. Indeed it is the preachers job to open up the text as God has written it, and it is the Holy Spirits job to open up the heart and the mind to reveal what God wants to be revealed at any given time. Neither should we doubt whether God has or even can preserve his Word. Let's just take a much more simple approach, and dare I say it a more child-like approach. If God indeed has spoken into real time history, and if he has indeed created a whole universe by the breath of his words; and if we do actually believe him to be who he says he is then, I say again let us not doubt whether God can preserve his own Written and Inspired Words from the corruption of time and from evil machinations. As we saw from the Psalmist who is speaking directly concerning the Words of God: "Thou shalt keep them O Lord, Thou shalt preserve them from this generation, forever." (Psalm 12:7). He either can and has preserved his Word or he cannot and hasn't preserved his Word, it really is that simple.

We then went on to exhort those who think themselves called of God to preach as Paul exhorted Timothy "Preach the Word, in season and out of season". We showed that changing culture has no bearing whatsoever upon the message. As Noah preached, as Enoch peached, as Moses preached, as Samuel preached, as the Prophets preached, as John the Baptist preached, as the disciples preached, as Jesus himself preached, as the early Church Fathers preached, as the evangelists and the reformers preached, as every single preacher and pastor has preached for the last two thousand years so too must today's preacher and evangelist preach. It was John Wesley who declared to his fellow evangelists as they were set apart for the task of evangelising the length and breadth of the United Kingdom "fear nothing but God and sin." And off they went with hearts burning declaring to the "valley of dry bones" in which they lived, and into the culture in which they lived "flee from the wrath to come." (Matthew 3:7). Theirs and our message must be "repent and be baptised...in the name of Jesus Christ for the remission of sins, and ye shall receive the gift of the Holy Ghost...Save yourselves from this untoward generation." (Acts 2:38,40). "Believe upon the Lord Jesus Christ and Thou shalt be saved." (Acts 16:31). Along with these admonitions to the lost the preacher must also seek by God's good grace to preach the whole counsel of God to the assembly of saved believers, seeking to build them up in the most Holy Faith, resisting and rejecting science, cultural influences and the devils temptations to be adding to or taking away from the Word of The Lord.

We have also sought to encourage the preachers to handle God's Word faithfully, sincerely and without deception. The apostle Paul took great pains and made great efforts to not be among that crowd who corrupted God's Word. There were many in his day, as there have been down the aeons of time that have sought to twist, deceive, corrupt and to pervert the Word of God by adding to or to taking away from the revealed truth. The pressure to do this in our day is building up year on year. Even in the western culture formerly very much influenced by Christian truth, morals and ethics, even in our culture where great works of God have been achieved, where revival after revival has established and changed entire families, communities and nations, even here laws have been passed to silence the Christian. A growing number of preachers and pastors have found themselves the wrong side of those laws, they have lost their jobs and their livelihoods, they have been fined and imprisoned and they have been hounded by the mob of angry 'victims' to which they have sought to bring the gospel message of eternal salvation by Jesus Christ.

Under such pressures it is easy to give in and to compromise, I have seen such a compromise with my own eyes and heard it with my own ears, but I would urge any in who's hands these few words might happen to fall, and I would echo the words of the apostle Paul in Romans chapter 12: 1-2 " I beseech you therefore brethren, by the mercies of God, that ye present your bodies a living sacrifice, holy, acceptable unto God, which is your reasonable service. And be not conformed to this world: but be ye transformed by the renewing of your mind, that ye may prove what is that good, and acceptable and perfect will of God." In that word "be not conformed to this world," I heard one godly pastor say "don't let the world squeeze you into it's mould." This is exactly what is happening, all these pressures are working together to try and squeeze the Christian into the worlds mould and render him or her completely useless, silenced and weak while the world screams and shouts and carries on it's hell-bound course in wild abandonment.

And finally, in the light of what we have sought to teach it has been an inevitable outcome of our subject matter to exhort the readers of these pages to a serious, prayerful and genuine self examination of our standing before God. Painful though necessary, I trust that the motive and the spirit in which these words have come is understood to be one of love for the brethren and honour for the cause of Christ upon the earth. The question throughout these pages has always been "Who is on the Lord's side?" (Exodus 32:26). It is a question that I pray does not offend those who consider themselves 'called of God' to preach, or 'set apart' to pastor a church. I trust we are on biblical ground in asking for a humble self examination. Brethren, look into the divine record as it mirrors your heart, look for the evidence and let God be judge and jury, not me.

We have to change course and we have to offer again our bodies and our whole lives back into the hands of our God as "a living sacrifice, holy and acceptable to God." It is said of "the children of Ephraim, being armed, and carrying bows, turned back in the day of battle. They kept not the covenant of God. And refused to walk in his laws, and forgot his works, and his wonders that he had shown them." (Psalm 78:9-11). Have we turned back in the day of our battles? They were armed and ready but they turned back!! How discouraging for the rest of the army when a whole tribe suddenly ups and turns around and runs away. War is a fearful thing and as they stood there thinking over the forthcoming battle it began to overwhelm them and from one persons cries fear quickly spread through their ranks and they left their 'brothers in arms' to fight for themselves a whole tribe short. Interestingly the Psalmist says also that "they kept not the covenant of God, they refused his laws, they forgot his wonderful works." This wasn't just fear gripping the soul as they faced a terrifying enemy but it was seen as a rejection of God himself. They were guilty of breaking their covenant with God, they were guilty of not trusting their Lord and God who had wrought great and powerful deliverances in the past. They were not believing this and basically they were guilty of apostasy and refused to walk in God's law.

The things of which I have been speaking are all about rejecting God and removing the ancient boundary stones and historical foundational truths; rejecting, compromising and being unfaithful to God's written word, but now we must seek to encourage both people and preacher alike to arise from their current lethargy and fear, to turn again and face the battle. Let us look now at turning the tide and experiencing some sort of mighty restoration to the glory of God, and making our stand with myriads that have gone before us, men and women of God: heroes of the Faith indeed.

Getting Back Our Zeal and Contending for the Faith

"The zeal of thine house hath eaten me up."
(John 2:17) (Psalm 69:9)

Squaring the Circle

Contrary to popular Christian opinion Jesus was not always exhibiting those gentler characteristics of love and divine affection. On a number of occasions he was clearly, visibly and openly angry. This should not be of any surprise to those Christians who firstly, believe in the deity of Christ, who secondly, read their bibles, and who thirdly are born-again, bible believing Christians. The above text appears when the disciples experience Jesus making an actual whip and physically attacking people, turning over their tables and driving out the money changers in the temple. In Marks account of this repeated event he declares that "My house shall be called of all nations a house of prayer, but ye have made it a den of thieves." (Mark 11:17). The disciples also "remembered that it was written," (John 2:17) that it had been prophesied in that 69th psalm verse 9 that the zeal for God's house eats up the Messiah. Being eaten up by zeal is strong language indeed and we are dealing with extremely strong emotions, fiery emotions and an angry countenance. The sight of what was going on in the name of God consumed the beloved Jesus. The very place where prayer, meditation and worship should be taking place was now a market place of thievery and corruption, and Jesus acted. Now was a time of action not words only. You could say that now was a time of war not of peace, a time for battle not of waiting for the sound of the trumpet. Battle lines were being clearly drawn between the rulers of the temple and what was God's will, between religious hypocrisy and faithfulness, between false religion and the truth. I say that the battle lines were being drawn because this event happened twice, once at the beginning of Jesus' ministry and once near the end. The event recorded in

Johns Gospel is at the beginning and this is where the Lord was laying down a marker, a warning and a message that "a greater than the temple stood in their midst," and the one who stood and spoke did so with all the authority of the Godhead. How dare they, therefore allow such blasphemy to be acted out in God's house and in God's name.

Another point regarding these incidents of Jesus cleansing the temple is the fact that they are recorded in all four gospels. Every writer of the gospel was moved by, and inspired by the Holy Spirit to record the events for our learning and instruction. Make no mistake about it, this was an important event and must not be missed out of the inspired narrative. If this is the case then what does it mean? What can we learn? How does this apply in our historical context? I personally cannot remember one sermon preached upon this text. I might be mistaken or I might have forgotten, but be that as it may if I did hear a sermon on this passage it was only once or twice and it must not have been very memorable! I think you would agree this subject isn't really a 'go to' subject for the pastors and bible teachers, and the reason I believe is once again many church leaders simply cannot or will not understand the Jesus they try and portray and the Jesus in the text, so they avoid it. We are back to our 'evangelical snowflake' mentality again. A Jesus that makes a whip and starts attacking people, and a Jesus that overturns tables and literally forces people against their will to leave the temple isn't the Jesus they believe in, want to understand, or even preach about. The modern church fears the lessons that might be learned from Jesus' cleansing the temple and the practical consequences for us as those lessons are applied and therefore completely shies away from dealing with the issue.

Another reason why this text is rarely, if ever preached upon is I would suggest that the modern 'snowflake evangelical' just cannot square the circle between God's love and his wrath, between Jesus' grace and his justice. They know nothing, or very little of inward necessity, of having a deep felt burden, of having a fiery zeal and of experiencing a spiritual passion that painfully consumes them. They cannot understand these things because of all that has been previously said in this book. This is the fruit of the near total removal of those fundamental, foundational boundary stones and ancient landmarks of which I have been saying. The Jesus they continue to portray is a false Jesus, a half a Jesus. He is a Jesus built upon nothing but one from their own imagination and their own humanistic reasoning, interested only in making people better and concerned only for some social justice. If one rejects the old testament and thus it's foundational teaching, and if one doubts, denies and shies away from the God revealed in the old testament then you build only with "wood, hay and stubble" an edifice which will be blown away at the first storm and burned up at the inspection of Almighty God. (1 Corinthians 3:10-15). This is a house built upon sand and not upon the rock. (Matthew 7:24-27). It is at precisely this point that every wind of false doctrine, weakness and worldliness enters the church and "every man does that which is right in his own eyes." (Judges 21:25). Everything becomes tolerated, all things become open for debate, there is nothing that cannot be brought to the table to be questioned and doubted and there is no past evangelical, protestant, fundamental truth once held firm for two thousand years that cannot be caste aside in the name of changing culture, progressive values and modern ideology. Many modern pastors and church leaders are completely taken in by these liberal delusions and thus have nothing really to offer, they have no fight and no zeal whatsoever, and like I said just do not understand what is going on and cannot, in their hearts and minds, square this circle. This spirit of compromise and apostasy is exactly what Jesus faced when he entered the temple and when the Pharisees came to question him. But let us continue.

Jesus' Anger and Zeal

The Lord Jesus time and time again faced the Pharisees head on and gave them not a single inch in the debate. If they were willing to sit down and reason he would do so, but unfortunately this was not often the case, they were constantly trying to catch him at his words, to upset him, accuse him falsely, blaspheme him, undermine his authority, twist the word of God and keep the poor souls under their care bound in some type of false Jewish tradition and fear. He would have non of it and he did not fear them or their threats one single bit. In Luke 11:37-54 in the house of a Pharisee that had invited him to eat he made a blistering attack upon them. In this passage he calls them fools and hypocrites and accuses them of murder; he exposes their deeds as futile, meaningless and false. In a similar passage in Matthew chapter 23 he uses the same language: fools and hypocrites, and he also adds blind and blind guides, serpents and generation of vipers. In another place he calls them children of the devil. (John 8:44). If we add to this the account in all four Gospels of Jesus cleansing the temple, (Matthew 21:12,13, Mark 11:15-19, Luke 19:45-48, John 2:14-17) we can see quite clearly that Jesus being righteously angry was not a one off or him somehow acting out of character. There are numerous instances in the gospels where the Lord of glory lays into the religious hypocrites of his day, and like I said he gives them 'no quarter' at all, he makes no apology and he justifies nothing which he says regarding the religious leaders who held their office in corruption and lies.

If Jesus was alive today and ministering throughout the land I have no doubt whatsoever that the Christian leaders would despise him and want him 'cancelled' and killed. The Church of England and all the other major Christian denominations would receive the same censure, he would expose their unbelief of the scriptures, their twisting of the scriptures, and their complete absorption of the atheistic, secular and 'post truth' culture. He would stand for non of their traditions and pretended Christianity. At least he could say of the Pharisees that they had a righteousness regarding the keeping of the Law (Matthew 5:20) but nowadays the Church of England especially holds no moral authority whatsoever for not only have they steered away from their once held evangelical tenets but they also for example accept homosexuals in the pulpit. Christ would not stand for such hypocrisy from men holding themselves up as some Christian leader, moral guide and spiritual confidant while being so far removed from simple, basic Christian living. Jesus' anger and zeal would break out upon them and they would hate him for it as did the majority of the Jewish rulers of his day.

We see also this Christian zeal throughout the new testament and we shall look at a couple of examples.

Apostles Peter and John

Being eaten up by a fiery zeal wasn't exclusive to Jesus nor should it be, and remember I am thinking primarily of the leaders and the preachers amongst God's people. These are the ones who should be leading the line, forging forward into battle and leading by example, bringing the flock of Christ with them. Not long after the resurrection, as the church was just beginning to gain some momentum and many souls were being added to their number Peter and John were arrested. In Acts 3 we find them preaching the everlasting gospel and an impotent man was miraculously healed. In Acts 4 we see them apprehended by the religious authorities "and as they spake unto the people, the Priests, the captain of the Temple and the Sadducee's came upon them, being grieved that they taught the people, and preached through Jesus the resurrection from the dead. And they laid hands on them and put them in the hold.." (Acts 4:1-3). It didn't take long before the preaching of the Apostles got them into trouble with these religious hypocrites. What has to be noted here first of all is their transformation from fearful cowards and deniers of Jesus to men willing to stand in the public square of testimony. Not a few weeks earlier they all ran away and hid themselves, scattering as their beloved head shepherd was struck down, but now we see a different animal entirely. Now we see boldness; now we see zeal, and now we see an unmovable and steadfast spirit. Now these men could look these Pharisees squarely in the eye and declare "Ye rulers of the people, and elders of Israel...be it known unto you all, and to all the people of Israel that by the name of Jesus Christ of Nazareth, whom ye crucified, whom God raised from the dead...doth this man stand here before you all...Neither is there salvation in any other: for there is non other name under heaven given among men whereby we must be saved." (verses 10-12). These few but simple words struck right at the very heart of everything the religious leaders stood for and Peter and John showed no fear whatsoever in declaring the truth. They knew it could cost them their lives; they knew that they too could be crucified like their master but zeal for the kingdom had eaten them up. The Pharisees convened together "and saw the boldness of Peter and John...they called them and commanded them to not speak at all, nor teach in the name of Jesus." (verses 13,18). A rule came from this scholarly and august assembly of Israel's finest to no longer speak or teach in the name of Jesus; surely this would stop them in their tracks; surely this would engender the old fear in their hearts; surely this would cause a capitulation of these men and a collapse of the cause. They were sadly mistaken for these men were full of the Holy Ghost (verse 8) and thus full of zeal "but Peter and John answered and said unto them, whether it be right in the sight of God to hearken unto you more than unto God, judge ye. For we cannot but speak the things that we have seen and heard." (verses 19-20).

Peter and John weren't getting into some sort of theological debate with these men; there was to be no religious discussion whatsoever, there was just a holy boldness and zeal and a complete rejection of the authority of all those religious leaders. "You judge what is right or wrong before God, you do what you want to do and think what you want to think, but we are carrying on doing what we want to do and what God has called us to do, you have no authority here," is what they said. There would be no capitulation today and there would be no compromise, no debate or discussion just obedience to the Word of God and to the call of God. But let us look at another example.

The Apostle Paul
In the book of Galatians we see Paul both zealous and angry but equally holy and just. The back-ground to Paul's letter is that false teachers had crept in and were infringing upon the new-found Christian liberties of the Galatians. The main issue was regarding circumcision, these false teachers were claiming that the converted Gentiles had to be circumcised to be saved and Paul right from the start whilst explaining the true Christian position doesn't compromise or debate the issue. True truth is thundered forth taking no prisoners.

He begins by declaring his amazement at their departure from the faith, "I marvel that you are so soon removed from him that called you into the grace of Christ unto another gospel." (Chapter 1:6). Right from the very beginning he calls these false teachers doctrine "another gospel" and declares vehemently "though we, or an angel from heaven, preach any other gospel unto you than that which we have preached unto you, let him be accursed." (verse 8) And as if the Holy Spirit wished to drive home this point he says again in the very next verse "as we said before, so I say again, if any man preach any other gospel unto you than that ye have received, let him be accursed." "That wasn't very loving was it calling down curses upon people? Paul wasn't a very kind man name calling like that? He wont win many over to the cause with such negative and divisive language like that? They say he is a man of God and an apostle but he speaks to people in such a way! Where is the love? He's not very inclusive is he? He sounds like a religious bigot to me." This is exactly what the churches would say of him today, I know that from personal experience and from the testimony of others who speak the truth. But Paul wasn't finished there, he says that he wished that these false teachers would be "cut off that trouble you". (chapter 5:12). The actual meaning is that he wished that they might cut themselves off, a graphic illustration of self mutilation. He was angry and he was zealous and did not pull any punches but let his antagonisers have it straight between their metaphorical eyes.

There are many other occasions where this mighty apostle exuded such passionate zeal, one being regarding Elymas in Acts 13:8-11. Here was a "sorcerer" who was resisting the gospel and actively seeking to "turn away the deputy from the faith." Paul would not tolerate such open defiance without a fight, and on discerning the situation looked this devils disciple square in the face and the divine record says "then Saul (which is also called Paul) filled with the Holy Ghost, set his eyes on him, and said, O full of subtlety and all mischief, thou child of the devil, thou enemy of all unrighteousness, wilt thou not cease to pervert the right ways of the Lord? And now behold the hand of the Lord shall be upon thee, thou shalt be blind, not seeing the sun for a season." (verse 9-11). Let us just stop here and think for a moment upon this, for I fear that on more occasions than we realise we read over these passages without comprehending the actual events, or words, or even consider their application. Remember that Galatians passage where Paul curses those who would preach another gospel, well here he actually and by divine will brings down such a curse on a devil worshipper. He tells him directly what he is and what his character is: Evil! How do we fare when faced with such open resisting of the gospel? Would we dare to use such language if we were faced by Satan's disciples? I'm afraid in our day (and again I speak from personal experience) today's pastors and church leaders are much more fierce against God's own people if they imagine a perceived offence committed. They show zero discernment and 100% misplaced rebuke. Their wolf-like character breaks through their sheep's clothing easy enough! But put them in the world and they purr like a little pussy cat, friends with everyone! Paul however, "full of the Holy Ghost," had much better discernment than modern Christendom has, and when he saw that the truth was at stake and thus the honour of God and of Christ; and when he comprehended the fundamentals beginning to be denied and foundational stones being removed he knew that the whole edifice would collapse, becoming no gospel at all just a hazy, fuzzy quasi-religious morality of a works based salvation that will save no one but will damn anyone caught up in it's treacherous web of lies and deceit. We absolutely need to get back our zeal and we absolutely need to show from time to time a holy, righteous anger against heresy and false Christianity.

We have looked a little at Jesus, Peter and John, and the Apostle Paul but what of those who might be walking precariously close to the edge of this carnal precipice? What of those in whose hands this book might fall? What of those who's hearts the Lord has touched and feel themselves beginning to arise? What of those who wish to change and fight in the Lord's battles but feel themselves weak and weary? Well to such souls I would ask a question:

Is There Not a Cause?
Goliath of Gath was mocking the Israelites and the God of Heaven and he stood as their champion to defy the armies of Israel and non would dare fight this giant, animal of a man. David came to bring food for his brothers who were with Saul's army and as he heard Goliath defying God, his anger and his spirit was stirred up "who is this uncircumcised

Philistine, that he should defy the armies of the living God." (1 Samuel 17:26). Eliab, David's brother was angry with David and accused him falsely "...why camest thou down hither?..I know thy pride and the naughtiness of thine heart; for thou art come down that thou mayest see the battle." (verse 28). It is at this point David stood his ground to his elder brother and said "What have I done now? Is there not a cause?" (verse 29). I would ask the same question, and I would dare to ask church leaders, pastors and preachers, is there not a cause? Never mind about throwing around false accusations like Eliab, answer the question! Look at the world, look at the English church, look at our congregations and the new 'evangelical snowflake', and ask yourself again is there not a cause?

Issues in the church are not dealt with neither are all the issues in the world; the ever increasing weight of godlessness and vile carnality is now pressing in upon us. We have completely capitulated to liberal false shepherds and now we feel that we have nothing within to fight against the secular and humanistic onslaught, and as we have come away from our fundamental moorings the weakness of the church is all the more apparent, and year by year we are falling more under the influence of the diabolical spell of "the god of this world." (1 Corinthians 4:4). Is there not a cause? Every year the law seems to strengthen against the freedom to preach the whole gospel, I say the whole gospel because one would only have to mention certain subjects and certain communities and the police will be knocking at your door with questions about a 'hate crime' having been committed. Even in the churches there now appears many taboo subjects, which when preached upon the so-called Christians walk out of meetings because they have been offended at the truth. All this muzzles the pastor who becomes afraid to lose his congregation and thus his livelihood. The Muslim community, Black Lives Matter, Climate Change activists, the LBGT+ community and every other minority group all have more fire, and more zeal and more sense of a cause than the church does. Where is our protest? Where is our unity? Where is our zeal for the kingdom of God? Is there not a cause?

"Now while Paul waited for them at Athens, his *spirit was stirred in him*, when he saw the city wholly given to idolatry. Therefore disputed he in the synagogue of with the Jews, and with devout persons, and in the market daily with them that met with him." (Acts 17:16,17). Firstly, let it be noted that the exact same expression is used here as we saw with David, "his spirit was stirred." Something was happening both spiritually and physically. This was something definite, an emotion, a feeling, a burden which was a physical phenomenon. It was so strong an emotion that it produced a crying out, it produced action, a fight and a going on the attack, it could not be held back and could not be stopped. And thus Paul's spirit stirred whilst he was waiting for Silas and Timotheus to come to him at Athens (verse 15). As he waited we are told that "his spirit was stirred within him.." He was looking at all the idolatry that was going on; he saw all that superstition, hundreds, perhaps thousands completely blinded by blocks of wood and pieces of stone. He himself had the answer to all this rampant idolatry and his soul became deeply troubled, so troubled that he could not withhold himself any longer, he must speak, he must reason and he must dispute with any who would listen. Notice however he didn't just dispute with those idolaters, he went first to the synagogue, to the Jews, to the church in his day. Here he first sought to reason then he seeks to reason with the rest of the ordinary folk around him, in the market place. Here, questions need to be asked. Does our spirit get equally stirred from time to time? Or do we feel nothing when we see the world around us in it's lostness or the church in it's apostasy? Is there not a cause? Jude exhorts his hearers to "earnestly contend for the faith, which was once delivered unto the saints." (verse 3). The reason he gives for this absolutely necessary contending is in the very next verse, "for certain men crept in unawares...ungodly men, turning the grace of God into lasciviousness, and denying the only Lord God, and our Lord Jesus." The ongoing message from Jude was to "earnestly contend;" the church was under attack by "ungodly men" denying the faith, doubting the faith, undermining the faith, corrupting the faith and seeking to infect others with their spiritual disease, the time now was to go on the offensive, on the attack, into battle and donning the full armour of God. The time was to be merciless with these hypocrites and heretics thrusting the sword of the Spirit, which is the word of God right into the heart of their demonic ideologies. When the truth is at stake and when our dear brothers and sisters in the Lord are being led astray, and for the honour of our God and his kingdom a stand has to be made, and the Lords chosen pastors, preachers and church leaders are to lead the line, and the rest of the flock follow on behind.

We Are All Warriors Now
This zeal and warrior spirit should be a mark of as many as the Lord's people as possible and not just the leadership. Does not the Apostle Paul encourage all to put on the whole armour of God? "Finally my brethren, be strong in the Lord and in the power of his might. Put on the whole armour of God, that ye may be able to stand against the wiles of the devil." (Ephesians 6:10-11). That word "brethren" means brothers and sisters and is an exhortation from the Apostolic leadership to all the rest of the people of God. Non are exempt from this fight and all are required to take their place within the assembly of the saved. Paul looks at the Roman soldier and re imagines what the Christian should look like and how he or she should stand before the world of principalities and powers. Indeed, if one does not stand as a soldier on the spiritual battlefield then you will be taken captive by the devil at his will, who will seek to destroy you completely, and totally ruin your testimony and thus the honour of belonging to Christ. These exhortations of

Paul are imperatives; they are mandatory not obligatory. We all will have our personal battles to fight on our way to the celestial city and a fighting, zealous spirit is an absolute necessity for we are told "be sober, be vigilant, because your adversary the devil as a roaring lion walketh about, seeking whom he may devour. Whom resist steadfast in the faith…" (1 Peter 5:8-9). This vigilance, soberness and resisting are qualities that carry with them zeal, fight and a holy anger which we all should exhibit. Nobody ever fought successfully who could not summon up some level of anger for the enemy which stands before them, and our enemy as the scriptures declare is subtle, cruel, violent, deceitful and very real. Our wrestle is real, our battlefield is real and the spiritual realm is real and the sooner we realise this the better for us. We have to prepare by immersing ourselves in God's Word and by being men and women of intercession and prayer. Interestingly, after Paul has described the armour that we should put on in Ephesians chapter 6:14-17, he exhorts that all should be covered in prayer, "praying always with all prayer and supplication in the Spirit, and watching thereunto with all perseverance and supplication for all saints." (verse 18). Fellowship with God is what binds the armour of God together.

Thus armed and equipped the Christian has a responsibility to stand for truth and justice, in love and grace, by the power of the Holy Spirit. He takes his position within the church of Jesus Christ praying that he shall be a blessing in it, and he stands before a fallen world seeking to squeeze us into its mould. He prays that God might use him with the gifts that he is pleased to grant him, and he guards the honour of Christ and the honour of the "Bride of Christ" even with his life if that is required. He does all this seeking to live at peace with all men, not deliberately antagonising those around him nor with those with whom he has to work. This holy collective is to advance and go forward in every age and in every culture with steely determination preaching to all flesh that Jesus alone is "Saviour, Christ and Lord." (Luke 2:11). When he falls (and he will) he arises; when he sins he repents; when he is weary he calls upon God; when he is victorious he is to be humble for it is God that has empowered him not he himself, and it is God alone that can preserve him and keep him until he passes from this world into the next. This will happen when he fights his last battle with death itself, but he knows that his Lord and Master has gone before him mightily conquering that final foe. "O death where is thy sting? O grave where is thy victory? The sting of death is sin. And the strength of sin is the law. But thanks be to God which giveth us the victory through our Lord Jesus." (1 Corinthians 15:55-57).

Mothers in Israel
Some might think that all this talk of war and battling, of fighting and of zeal etc. might not have a ready ear amongst the women in our churches. Even though I do think men are more naturally given to this type of language, this spiritual warfare is just that a spiritual reality not a physical one, and one that all God's people are to be enlisted in. We are not dealing with bravado and a kind of Alpha Male macho-ism, but rather we are talking of a strength of character and purpose, and a personal fighting spirit that transcends gender stereotypes. The scriptures are replete with tremendous encouragements of women of God who themselves fought the Lord's battles and exerted such a holy zeal and fire that not only gives great honour to their Lord Jesus but gives great honour to women also.

In 2 Samuel chapter 20 we read of Joab chasing after Sheba an insurrectionist and "a man Belial," who declared "we have no part in David, neither have we inheritance in the son of Jesse." (verse 1). Joab, David's commander of the armies of the Lord pursues Sheba who takes refuge in a city Abel (verse 15) and begins to besiege it. But a wise women (we are not told her name) to save the city from complete destruction shouts to Joab over the wall "I am one of them that are peaceable and faithful in Israel: Thou seekest to destroy a city and a mother in Israel: why wilt thou swallow up the inheritance of the Lord?...Behold his head (Sheba's) will be thrown to thee over the wall." (verses 19-21). Here we have a wise woman and a women that understood the times in which she lived. She recognised David as the rightful King and consequently rejected the anarchy of Sheba. She thus sought to save the city with many hundreds of people and give Joab what he wished for the dead body of Sheba. She knew what was required. She arranged that Sheba be given up and his head taken off his shoulders, this was the will of God. Here we have a true "mother in Israel," a woman of God and a woman who exemplified the necessary zeal for the cause of the kingdom. We have a rightful king, Jesus, and there are many who would seek to usurp his authority, no quarter must be given. There is no room at all for insurrectionists or spiritual anarchists within the assemblies of God's people. We serve a greater David, even Jesus who alone receives all the glory and adulation befitting a "King of Kings."

In the days of the Judges, and chapter 4 of that book, another rebel against the people of God met his end by the hand of a woman, Sisera by name who was the captain of the army of Canaan. He had oppressed the children of Israel for 20 years (verse 2,3). Again, being pursued by the armies of Israel he alone was left and he went weary into the tent of Jael the wife of Heber, (verse 17). Jael subtly coerced Sisera into her tent "turn in my lord, turn in to me, fear not." (verse 18). And once he had fallen asleep "Jael, Heber's wife took a nail of the tent, and took a hammer in her hand, and went softly unto him, and smote the nail into his temples and fastened it into the ground." (verse 21). What made these women act the way in this way? Answer, boldness and zeal for the kingdom and cause of Almighty God. These physical and actual events are pictures of the fighting spirit and spiritual character that is necessary to fight the Lord's spiritual battles in these days in which we live. False Christianity, false teachers and usurpers of Christ's glory must be rebuked and put to the spiritual sword, The Word of God. These two women were true "mothers in Israel" and knew what the times called for and no amount of sentimentality would appease the enemies of the Lord then or now.

The old testament scriptures also speak of Sarah, Rebekah, Rachel and Leah; of Deborah, Esther, Naomi and Ruth; of Hannah and of Hilda the Prophetess. In the new testament we hear of Anna at the temple, all the various Mary's, Lydia, Priscilla and the numerous other women mentioned at the end of Paul's epistles. Here we have a whole myriad of women of God who stood by Christ when others fled, who anointed him with their tears and who spoke of him to all who would listen. Here we have encourager's of the Lord, of the Apostles and of the saints in general; here we have a grand company of true womanhood, fearless, zealous and fighters in his kingdom. I would say to the women of our day, be like the old Viking Shield Maidens who fought alongside their men folk, not only were they mothers, daughters, sisters and wives but warriors for the cause. Fight alongside the men of the church not against them; fight alongside your husbands not against them. Take up the armour of God with the men folk and if we die on the battlefield together then so be it. The dust of the Colosseum has female blood mixed in it as well as men's; the ashes collected at the bottom of the burning stake has the ashes of brave, fearless women as well as that of men's. True biblical womanhood is rooted in truth, righteousness and justice as it is in love, grace and compassion. When you first heard the call of Christ to rise up and follow him then you became enlisted in your Lord's army. Follow those numerous biblical examples and take great heart that being on the Lord's side is to ultimately be on the winning side, though this might not be clearly evident in what we can see and hear in the physical realm. "We wrestle not against flesh and blood but against principalities, against powers, against the rulers of the darkness of this world, against spiritual wickedness in high places." (Ephesians 6:12).

Therefore, to those who some might consider "the weaker vessel" I say take up your armour and fight. Are the schools teaching your children and grandchildren things which they ought not, then fight it; do the authorities want to vaccinate your children against your will, then fight it; is there a tide of anti-christian ideology sweeping through your place of work, then fight it. Whatever and wherever the cause of Christ is to be found, in the home, the school, the street, the church, the workplace I say dear precious women of God and mothers in Israel, fight for your lives and your homes; fight for children and your grandchildren; fight for your God and King, no compromise and no surrender, emulate those wonderful women of God of which we read in God's own word.

What About Loving our Enemies and the Love of God?

Some might be thinking where is the love of God in all this? "Are we not told to love our enemies and bless those who persecute us? All this fighting and anger seems diametrically opposed to love, grace and mercy does it not? Surely we've moved on from all that anger and revenge, and this language has no place in the diverse Christian community today." At first these ideas of fighting heretics and loving our enemies might well appear to be contradictory, but the preacher is to be as Timothy whom Paul exhorted, "study to show thyself approved unto God, a workman that needeth not to be ashamed rightly dividing the word of truth." (2 Timothy 2:15). It is that phrase "rightly dividing the word of truth." From this we understand that there are no contradictions in God's Word only complimentary truths, we understand also that there are

Christian paradoxes, things which appear to be opposite truths but are indeed different sides of the same coin, and it takes one who is called of God, anointed of the Lord and one who is studying to show himself approved who shall be able to rightly divide this word of truth.

So, is there a contradiction in Jesus who himself declared "love your enemies" but then proceeded to make "a whip of cords and drove out the money changers,"? Do we see hypocrisy in him who was the embodiment of divine love and yet scolded the Pharisees: "hypocrites, brood of vipers, serpents, children of the devil, white washed sepulchres etc.?" There is no contradiction whatsoever because the love and grace of God doesn't mean that sin should not be exposed by the light of the truth. Indeed, we could say that it is explicitly the love of God that rebukes and exposes sin for what it is. It is divine love that convicts, that rebukes, that exhorts and that censures. Does not Paul tell us that it is the "goodness of God" that leads us unto repentance? (Romans 2:4). Does John not explain that when the Holy Spirit comes he shall first convict of sin? (John 16:8). Does the writer to the Hebrews not encourage us that God chastises those whom he loves? (Hebrews 12:6). Conviction of sin, repentance and chastisements are all painful experiences, but they are all necessary experiences, and are all experiences that stream directly from the love of God. God's harsh words and actions are the very thing that we need to hear and experience to lead us back to himself. God's justice compliments his love, and righteousness always compliments truth. Truth, justice, love, grace and mercy are not contradictory graces but complimentary attributes of a great, sovereign and a loving God. The Pharisees in being thus rebuked were not being chided from an angry vengeful spirit; Jesus never acted towards those Temple money changers in a rash, uncontrolled and volatile manner. Our Lord was in complete control and acted well within a spirit of holiness, justice and love. A harsh lesson? Yes, for those who felt the strike of the whip, but a just one nonetheless, for God's house was being desecrated. Better to be bruised, learn the lesson, and enter into heaven than be showered with false love, feel nothing and drop into hell. If God should spare the rod then all his children will remain spoiled, carnal and worldly, but let him strike us occasionally and we shall be saved from many hardships and perhaps even from hell itself. Imagine if I am a hypocrite or an evil twister of God's words, and imagine too if I should hear a message of rebuke and the doom which awaits those who commit such sins. Then on hearing the censure I have a chance to be saved, and I have a chance to be changed and to make my peace with the Lord. Do you think that I should have been left to just get on with what I was doing with no exposure, rebuke or conviction? Should I have been left alone to carry on my sin? It is sweet undeserved mercy and wonderful divine love that would chastise me and call me out and away from such a corrupted lifestyle. The Lord rebuked those Chief Priests etc. precisely because he loved them not because he desired to curse them.

The Apostle Paul himself was one such Pharisee and a shining light amongst those hypocrites but who got that second chance. He was rebuked of the Lord Jesus and was gloriously saved to live and work for him, becoming one of the main writers of the new testament and founding many churches across the middle east. Nicodemus who was also a Pharisee and "a ruler of the Jews" (John 3:1) and the one who questioned Jesus, after Jesus' death he "came and brought a mixture of myrrh and aloes...took the body of Jesus and wound it in linen clothes with the spices.." (John 19:39-40). How can we explain this change of heart and this act of love and concern? The very one whom Jesus declared "ye must be born-again" did indeed undergo the necessary saving transformation. While the other Pharisees and chief rulers rejoiced over Jesus' death Nicodemus mourned and gave

Christ the honour and respect that was due to the true Messiah, truly he had himself been born-again. The scriptures also record that "among the chief rulers many believed on him." (John 12:42). What grace is this, "many believed on him," even of those that he chastised sharply. What these scriptures tell us plainly is that there was no contradiction whatsoever between Jesus severely rebuking the religious leaders and many of them actually believing upon him. They needed to hear what they heard from Jesus, the truth had to be told and their sin of hypocrisy exposed. This was their pathway to be saved. Jesus loved them the most when he rebuked them the sharpest. And this is true of all those other new testament writers who under the inspiration of the Spirit rebuked and exposed false teachers and religious hypocrites. Only heaven will reveal how many of those false teachers and religious hypocrites finally were turned, changed and wondrously saved.

Think also for a moment of God's final and total judgement, has God not loved all those his enemies when he has caste them all into a lost, Christ-less, sinners hell? Are all those enemies of God subjects of God's hypocrisy, saying he loves them and then damning them? Again it is the love of God that has rebuked them for their sins in their earthly lives; it is love that has called them to faith and repentance whilst they roamed the earth, and it is divine love that God punished his own Son in their place, if they would but accept it and believe it. He offers all flesh eternal life every day that they live. He is not far from everyone of us, but in him we live, and move, and have our very being. (Acts 17:27-28). God is patient and delays his justice from swiftly descending upon mankind out of love. Indeed as Nehemiah records "...but thou art a God ready to pardon, gracious and merciful, slow to anger, and of great kindness..." (Nehemiah 9:17). With this Joel agrees "...rend your heart and not your garments, and turn unto the Lord your God: for he is gracious and merciful, slow to anger, and of great kindness..." (Joel 2:13). The Lord is "slow to anger;" he gives men time and space to change, to turn and to repent. Remember he would not have even destroyed that vile place Sodom and Gomorrah if there were but ten righteous souls dwelling there. The global deluge was thousands of years in the making as Noah and Enoch preached to the wicked men of that time. Time and time again Moses pleads with the hard hearted Pharaoh to let his people go, and to his own people he sent prophet after prophet to turn them from their stubbornness and sin. In all these instances God stayed his hand, but by and by mercy must give way to justice and the Lord descends to take vengeance upon his enemies and upon those who refuse to listen and turn that they might be saved. In the last days God will also withhold his wrath as long as his providence will allow. Speaking of the fiery overthrow and the promise of Christ's second coming many will mock "saying, where is the promise of his coming," but Peter tells us that "the Lord is not slack concerning his promise, as some men count slackness; but is long suffering to us-ward, not willing that any should perish, but that all should come to repentance." (1 Peter 3:4,9). So we see clearly that God's justice is slow to appear for he pleads for men to turn to him in repentance and faith. He is not willing that millions drop into an eternal hell but rather waits for more to enter into the Ark, this indeed is true love.

Now, these attributes of mercy and justice are perfectly seen in the Lord Jesus, and the fact that Jesus expressed both of these attributes in the flesh, in his ministry reveals that "in him dwelleth all the fulness of the Godhead, bodily." (Colossians 2:9). In our text he was angry, but perfectly so, and it was a holy, perfect anger for his Fathers house, "zeal for thine house hath eaten me up." (John 2:17). The rulers had made the house of God a market place and a "den of Thieves," when it was supposed to be "a house of prayer for all nations." (Mark 11:17). What a contrast; a place for contemplation, prayer, intercession and communion with God was now a place where the corrupted money changers plied their trade. The world had entered the church, the secular had replaced the sacred, and the carnal dominated the holy. As we have been discussing the gradual moving away from the fundamentals in these studies, and as we look out at the church in our day, what is our reaction? How do we feel when the things of God are trampled upon by the religious leaders of our day? When we see the foundational stones being shifted from their traditional positions and when we hear the continual denial of the fundamentals of the faith, how does it affect us? When the pastors and church leaders do not even care about the bibles they have their hands or which they teach from, or even what is in the hands of their congregations, what do we think? When these same pastors avoid large sections of the word of God for not wanting to offend or upset folk, again how do we feel about it? Why do church leaders appear to not care less about the catastrophes in the world and the impact upon the people of God? When economic meltdown hits, or when earthquakes and pandemics strike the world, why again do our preachers completely fail in giving those biblical answers and divine comforts? "What saith the scriptures?" Shame on them all!! In short where is our zeal and where is our righteous anger? Where is the stirring of our soul? Do we not feel anything at all? Or are we completely content in our own 'safe space?' The only anger they seem to express is against those very people who point out these things. Oh yes, then out comes the sword when their foolish pride has been hurt. But for the zeal of which I speak and in its right place I contend the church has lost it, and we need to get it back pretty quickly.

But in getting back our zeal and fighting spirit, and in contending for the faith there is one last thing that we should consider.

A Warning

When James and John saw that a particular village of the Samaritans did not receive Jesus they were non too pleased and said to Jesus "Lord, wilt thou that we command fire to come down from heaven and consume them, even as Elias did?" But he turned and rebuked them, and said "Ye know not what manner of spirit ye are of. For the Son of Man is not come to destroy men's lives but to save them." (Luke 9:54-56). Here we have two men zealous for the Lord of Hosts, and here we have two men that thought they could read the will of God in his will to either judge or to save. They were zealous for the cause of Christ but their zeal was severely misplaced in that they wished that this whole village be burned up by the fiery judgement of God. They knew their old testament scriptures and drew upon the knowledge of Elijah in 2 Kings 1:9-12 when Ahaziah the King of Samaria commanded his men to come and get Elijah and bring him to him. On that occasion one hundred of his men were consumed by the fire of God. Here is an instance of taking an event from the scriptures, misapplying and misusing it to serve a misplaced purpose. We must ask what made God condemning the men of Ahaziah a right thing for God to do? And what made James and Peter wishing the same judgement upon the Samaritans a wrong thing to do?

Firstly, the situation and context was completely different. Ahaziah was a worshipper of devils and when he was sick he enquired "of Baal-zebub the god of Ekron" whether he would recover or not, (verse 1). This was a constant and wholesale rejection of the God of Israel and a clear acceptance of Satan himself. This was also a public and open apostasy from the message of God and his prophet Elijah. Here the King is mocking God and his truth by openly choosing Satanism. Not only that but he wished to kill God's prophet as is clear from that 15th verse when the Lord encouraged him to "go down with him, and be not afraid of him." In the case of the village of the Samaritans, yes they rejected Christ into their region but they had not yet heard the message of the gospel. Ahaziah however would have had his many chances to repent and turn at the preaching of Elijah but he rejected them all continually. These Samaritans had not yet passed over the threshold of total apostasy. Jesus was still about his ministry and he was just passing through. He was yet to die and rise again for those Samaritans and they were yet to hear the full gospel. In fact after Jesus' resurrection the disciples came around again to this very same village to offer the loving grace of God and salvation by Jesus Christ, as is recorded in Acts chapter 8. On experiencing great persecution the church was "scattered abroad throughout the regions of Judea and Samaria," and we are told "Philip went down to the city of Samaria and preached Christ unto them" and "preached the gospel in many cities of the Samaritans" (Acts 8:1-8,25). So we see, it was not over for these Samaritans and their surrounding areas, God had yet a plan of salvation for them. Added to this the scriptures also indicate a reason why they would not receive Jesus into their village "they did not receive him because his face (Jesus' face) was as though he would go to Jerusalem" (verse 53), and in that 51st verse it says the same "he steadfastly set his face to go to Jerusalem." So, part of their not receiving him was really due to Jesus himself not wanting to go there, and the overriding providence of God in Christ continuing his destiny with suffering and death.

Having seen the two completely different situations and the misapplication of James and John it is important for the preacher especially to be continually aware of this spiritual 'banana skin'. To burn, to judge and to destroy should never be the preachers first word upon what might be perceived rejection or even actual rejection and persecution. Jesus rebuked these men telling them that he had come "to save and not to destroy" (verse 56). We learnt earlier about the love of God in exposing and rebuking sin, and this should be the predominant grace that informs all that we do and say, when we do this we would avoid the mistake of James and John. The mistake they made however is an easy one to make when we are dealing with such emotions as zeal and standing for God, that's why this passage is here to encourage us away from a harsh and condemnatory spirit.

This dangerous, misplaced zeal was also a characteristic of Paul before he was converted and of the Pharisees in general. Paul tells us regarding the Pharisees that they "had a zeal for God, but not according to knowledge," (Romans 10:2) and of himself he declares that he was "a Hebrew of the Hebrews...a Pharisee, concerning zeal, persecuting the church." (Philippians 3:5,6). The zeal for God was very real but once again it was dangerous, deadly and misplaced, it was also completely without knowledge. Their zeal was grounded in anger alone, it did not have for its base the mercy and love of God, neither had in it an end in the saving and the blessing of lost souls. It only condemns, kills and destroys, it has no mercy. And this is exactly what we see in Paul before his conversion and of those Pharisees; not only did they have the very Son of God (their own awaited Messiah) murdered, but proceeded to persecute, silence and kill his followers also. This is what "zeal without knowledge" looks like, and this has to be guarded against every day in our speaking and standing for God, both preacher and people alike. The example of our Lord in the gospels in how and when he speaks is truly remarkable as well as totally perfect. Everything he did was always in its right context and at the right time. There was always perfect harmony in everything he was, and he it is that we should seek to emulate the most.

In the book of Galatians in that 5th chapter Paul speaks of those characteristics that should always flow out from the Christian, "but the fruit of the Spirit is love, joy, peace, long suffering, gentleness, goodness, faith, meekness, temperance: against such there is no law." These attributes are in contrast to what Paul describes as "the works of the flesh." These he says, are "adultery, fornication, uncleanness, lasciviousness, idolatry, witchcraft, hatred, variance, emulation, wrath, strife, seditions, heresies, envyings, murders, drunkenness, revellings and such like..." When we are not living and walking in the Spirit, and when we are not living obedient lives in fellowship with our Lord then the workings of the flesh will be more evident and more dominant, and in our context those qualities of hatred, variance, emulations, wrath and strife will replace the godly zeal and the holy righteous anger of which we have been trying to speak about. This is exactly what happened to James and John, and this is exactly how Paul used to live and how the Pharisees acted also. If we have those fruits of the Spirit underpinning all of our walk, all of our thinking and all of our acting then more often than not our zeal shall not be misplaced, and our rebukes shall not be dangerous and damaging. We shall avoid being condemnatory, cruel and harsh but our true motive shall be for the glory of God, the restoration of the wayward and the salvation of the lost.

As I have said the church has lost its zeal and its contending for the Faith, and if we are to regain any semblance of authority and usefulness we simply must get it back. We must also ensure that we are men of love and compassion so that our zeal and our fight is not misplaced, fleshly, cruel and hard hearted. For now our ministry is to "save and not to destroy." The scriptures tell us that "the righteous are as bold as a lion." (Proverbs 28:1). In boldness we must stand for truth and for Christ, his gospel and glory. The Apostle Paul sums up our position perfectly in 2 Corinthians 10:3-5 "for though we walk in the flesh, we do not war after the flesh: For the weapons of our warfare are not carnal, but mighty through God to the pulling down of strongholds; casting down imaginations and every high thing that exalteth itself against the knowledge of

God, and bringing into captivity every thought to the obedience of Christ."

A Christians Response to the Laws of the State When in Contradiction to the Law and Will of God

> "Let every soul be subject unto the higher powers. For there is no power but of God...whosoever therefore resisteth the power, resisteth the ordinance of God..."
> (Romans 13:1-2)

> "Then Peter and the other apostles answered and said, "we ought to obey God, rather than men.""
> (Acts 5:29)

A Capitulation?

During the recent Covid-19 pandemic crises the overwhelming majority of churches, at the request or imposition of the governments of the world closed their doors, stopped all their meetings, including prayer meetings and bible studies. The leaders of the said churches refused to visit their flocks, including the discouraged, the sick and the dying, because this to now became illegal to do so, and the church pastors gladly obeyed. As the world closed down so too did the assemblies of the Lord with very few exceptions. It seems that during a time of global catastrophe God wasn't needed!! The church leaders and pastors obeyed unreservedly appealing to the above quoted verses from Romans chapter 13 as justification for their actions. When the churches were allowed to open (at the governments command) they opened with numerous restrictions which seemed to change week on week. Everybody was to be sufficiently spaced apart, wear face masks but with no singing. There were to be no 'tea and biscuits', this was deemed far too dangerous! When singing was allowed, it was to be done quietly with as little exertion as possible so that all fear of spreading a virus was minimised at all costs. As the governments coercive vaccination program continued and most of the Christian community were first in the queue to receive the experimental vaccines things began (again at the governments command) to get back to normal. I'm sure that England's Arch Bishop of Canterbury, Justin Welby's assertion that "Jesus would have taken the vaccine" helped a fearful, non thinking Christian community to make up their minds! Slowly but surely as the governments restrictions eased a collective sigh could be heard amongst our church leaders as they continued to obey and eventually went back to "doing church" as they did before.

However, not all churches agreed with their respective governments impositions and continued to gather and meet together (illegally) whatever the consequences might be. They took for their guidance the second scripture quoted above (along with numerous others) to justify their active disobedience of the State. In many of these churches the police can be seen closing down any meetings taking place, arriving with vans, baton wielding officers, and in many countries with guns as well. Some repeat offenders churches had their entire buildings ring fenced and cut off. Many of these church leaders were fined on the spot or received court case appearances for their disobedience to these new State diktats. For these Christians and their leaders who led from the front this wasn't about Covid-19, the fear engendered or the regulations imposed. They saw a greater context: The whole idea of the relationship between Church and State. Perhaps this issue has for the first time been brought to the fore amongst the Christian community in our western cultural context.

I include this subject in this book because I have been specifically addressing a return to biblical Christianity and the preaching thereof. I have been speaking of taking back the narrative, being bold and making a stand for God and of casting off that weak, insipid snowflake mentality. It is perhaps no coincidence that whilst writing this book the Covid-19 pandemic (or Plandemic) engulfed the world and I saw before my eyes what can only be described as a massive wholesale capitulation by the Christian Church of every denomination. This weakness and fall, and this complete lack of zeal and an inability to offer a frightened world real answers became to me a terrible discouragement and distraction. It seemed to feed directly into everything I have been trying to say. If we remove those ancient foundational stones and fundamentals of the faith (which we have) then the church has nothing to offer, absolutely nothing. Our message has been nowhere during the pandemic. What a pathetic embarrassment that the only message we have is "close the doors and take the vaccine, it's what Jesus would have done!" The damage has already been done, many of our unvisited folk and those left alone have not returned to our churches, and no doubt they shall now be accused of "forsaking the assemblies" (Hebrews 10:25). But the reasons run a little deeper than most of our pastors can understand or even wish to try and comprehend, instead they exhibit the very thing of which I speak, being easily offended, narcissistic and unable to see the damage that their capitulation has done.

But let us try and gain some understanding of the above quoted texts not only in the context of Covid-19 but of a wider context considering what might happen in the future when those same impositions are made upon our assemblies, and of laying down those "old path" foundational stones, of preaching again the "whole counsel of God" and of getting back our lost zeal for God and making some type of biblically based stand, come-what-may.

A Contradiction?
Of the two groups mentioned above both appealed to the scriptures for their actions and both seem on a first casual reading to have a case. Can it be that the Word of God actually contradicts itself on this issue? Have we found a flaw in the divine record? Or is there a context that has been ignored by

the one party or the other who quotes either text to justify their actions before the Lord? Well, I have mentioned in previous studies in this book that the Word of God does not contain 'contradictions' only 'complimentary' scriptures. There is always a context to any verse or passages of scripture which must always be understood to gain an understanding upon the whole. Again, I would say that many of these so-called church leaders or pastors should know this already. Is it the case that just to quote a text out of it's context (in the Covid-19 situation) has become the easy thing to do for fear of reprisals and consequences upon disobedience to the State?

Let us ask another question. Should the State always be obeyed, in all situations and especially regarding any laws it might seek to impose upon the Church of Jesus Christ in any context? Let us look at that Romans 13 passage versus 1-7, it all seems pretty clear cut does it not? Well, let me first say that there are numerous passages in the Word of God that show very clearly that God's people did not always obey the State, the King, the authorities, the rulers etc. in all and every situation. Christians and Hebrews in the bible and throughout the centuries did not and never have given wholesale blind obedience to the State or its rulers, whether they be Kings, Queens, Pharaohs, Councils, Governments and magistrates. So the very premise of Romans 13 on which many modern snowflake pastors have hung their hats is entirely false to even start with! Just to quote Romans 13 as if that is the end of all debate and discussion (which I personally have heard a number of times during the pandemic both privately and from the pulpit) reveals one of a few things. Firstly, they are gripped with fear and cowardice regarding their own lives and livelihoods. Secondly, they don't really know their bibles, or do not really understand the basic principles of biblical interpretation and application. And thirdly, they are no pastors at all, only false shepherds and false teachers that do not belong anywhere near a pulpit despite how eloquent and forceful they appear. If any reading these pages have taken Romans 13 as a justification to a blind obedience to the State without any real explanation in the Covid context or any other context then you fall into one of those three situations above. There might be other reasons that flow out of those mentioned, but be that as it may there has definitely been a failure of biblical interpretation and application, comparing scripture with scripture.

Before we actually get into Romans 13 I just want to mention this point of apparent contradictions in God's Word. Some verses do indeed appear to say opposite things but on closer, prayerful inspection by those who can "rightly divide the word of truth" a clearer truth shall be manifested. Let me just offer a couple examples. David declares in the Psalms "do not I hate them, O Lord, that hate thee?" and again "I hate them with a perfect hatred" (Psalm 139:21-22). And yet Jesus exhorts us, "love your enemies, bless them that curse you, do good to them that hate you..." (Matthew 5:44). Paul tells us with divine authority that we are "justified by faith without the deeds of the law," and again "...a man is not justified by the deeds of the law." (Romans 3:28 & Galatians 2:16). And yet James declares with equal clarity that "...by works a man is justified and not by faith only." (James 2:24). Paul says to Timothy in 1 Timothy Chapter 4 verse 10 that "...we trust in the living God, who is the Saviour of all men, specially of those that believe." But any bible believing Christian understands clearly from other scriptures that this verse does not mean what it appears to say. These are just a few examples that first appear to show glaring contradictions, two statements saying the exact opposite things: hate your enemies, love your enemies: justified by faith alone, justified by works and not just faith. God saves all mankind (universal salvation)!! Now, my point and purpose here is not to explain away these apparent contradictions but merely to show that they do exist, and that we have just such a situation in our Romans 13 passage and other scriptures. "Be subject to the higher powers...they are of God...whoever resisteth the power resisteth God: and they that resist shall themselves receive damnation." (verses 1-2). Obey the State for they are instituted by God himself, to disobey the State is to disobey God himself. But let us take a closer look and in taking a closer look let us widen our lens to begin our inspection from Romans chapter 12. Let us continue.

From that 12th chapter Paul is speaking about our Christian behaviour, he is encouraging us and exhorting us how we ought to behave and to conduct ourselves in this world. This is absolutely key to understanding Romans 13. Please open your bible and take a look for yourself. From verse 1-2 Paul is teaching us how we should behave towards our God. In verses 3-8 he is teaching how we ought to behave with our giftings in the church; from verses 9-13 he exhorts us in our conduct towards our brothers and sisters in the Lord, and then he moves on in verses 14-21 showing how we should behave towards the unbelieving world and even those who hate us. Then in that Romans 13 he follows the same teaching showing how we should behave towards the State. He is talking about Christian conduct and Christian behaviour regarding rulers, magistrates, kings etc. He is saying, yes, they are instituted by God so do not be anarchists, do not rebel against the State, be good citizens, do not give the State a reason to arrest you or imprison you. And then he gives some very specific examples. Do not "practice evil" (verse 4) pay your "taxes" and "customs" (verse 6-7). Give the necessary "fear and honour" to whom it is due. (verse 7) Do not be disrespectful to those in authority. Brethren this is clearly about being a model citizen with regard to all those civil issues. "Practice no Evil," do not be defrauding, or brawling, or murdering anyone, or whatever other things "Evil" might be. Do not be an insurrectionist, pay your taxes, pay your customs, honour those above you, don't get into such trouble so that the sword of the law and of justice comes down upon you.

There are actually two more scriptures very similar to this one and can be found in Titus 3:1-2 and 1 Peter 2:13-17. Please look them up and compare them all side by side. In both of these other texts as with the Romans passage there is no mention whatsoever of anything to do with the Church, or the assembly of God's people, nothing about the worship of God, or prayer meetings, or evangelising the lost, nothing! There is nothing about the church closing its doors at the request of the State, of organising its affairs according to the rules of the land; nothing of being registered with the authorities and allowing government officials to determine if we are functioning legally and in accordance with the State etc. No, Paul and Peter are not advocating those things as biblical imperatives, it is clearly not in their minds or thinking whatsoever. If the Holy Ghost (the Divine Author) had wanted us to understand those scriptures in that way do you not think that in any of those three passages it would have been clearly laid out the concept of obeying the State regarding the church's functioning etc.? In fact the very opposite is taught as we shall see in a moment. Romans 13 and those other two passages which are all very similar are all about being good citizens in our respective countries, not acting in an evil way regarding the civil laws of the land, honouring those above us, paying our taxes and generally acting with good Christian character and not being anarchists or insurrectionists.

Remember also, that we are not talking about a world of 'rainbows and unicorns'. These Gentile and Jewish Christians were living in a place where hatred and persecution could spring up at any moment at the psychotic whim of the next Caesar. There were many rebels and insurrectionist at this time against the Roman State, and the Church, says Paul and Peter was to have no part whatsoever in that world, even as Jesus warned Peter any who take up the sword run the high risk of dying by the sword. Instead they encourage them to be good and godly citizens and pray for the welfare of those around them and of those in power. As I said he doesn't even mention the church and its functioning, and there is one very good reason for that, and it is this. The operating and the functioning, and the sheer existence of the church of Jesus Christ and their gathering together has nothing whatsoever to do with the Roman State or any other State anywhere, ever. The church doesn't even come under the jurisdiction of the State authorities, Kings, Queens, Governments etc. He understood, as did those Early Church Middle Eastern Christians that they are not subject to any man made law or human regulations regarding the church and functioning of the true body of Christ.

There are two more very good reasons why Paul doesn't even mention the church and whether it should be subject to the laws of the State and the first is that they already knew this truth as a living reality. Their everyday Christian experience was one of avoiding the authorities, they knew already that in this regard they were enemies of the State. They already met sometimes openly and sometimes in secret if necessary, the rules on whether they could open their church doors did not lie with the State, the rule of Caesar, the Pharisees or some other Judean Governor. The Roman Christians already knew that regarding their being practising Christians automatically meant that they were or could be seen as law breakers. The edicts of Caesar meant absolutely nothing to them; if they could meet freely without reprisals or persecution, they would; if they had to meet in secret because the State forbade them to meet they did; and if they had to go into the Roman Colosseum to face their death, they went freely being falsely accused as anarchists, insurrectionists and enemies of the State.

The second reason Paul probably doesn't mention it here is because it is mentioned elsewhere in the scriptures. In fact, it is such a common thread running right through the bible that Paul felt that it hardly needed reiterating here. This is Sunday school stuff and really should be a cause of deep embarrassment to those pastors and church leaders who have appealed to this scripture (and those others) as a justification to close their doors at the behest of the government regulations. It really does expose the foolishness and the fear of the modern, progressive snowflake pastors who have so much to lose when they claim Romans 13 authorises complete obedience in all things spiritual and holy. Close your doors, stop your preaching, stop your praying, stop your singing, in fact stop meeting together at all anywhere until we, 'The State', say so. OK, we bow to your supreme God-given commands! Friends, this not biblical Christianity, this is being tossed about with every wind of doctrine upon the high seas of fear, capitulation and ignorant acquiescence.

However, let us know look at some braver souls in the scriptures who know that regarding the things of God it is better to obey the Lord than the edicts of men. And might I also add that these passages we are about to look at really are the stuff of the Sunday School class, but we have come to such a state of affairs that such simple basic Christian teaching is almost completely lost on the modern leaders of our churches.

The Hebrew Midwives
We have all read the story or perhaps heard it from the pulpits how those Hebrew midwives refused to kill all the male children. Let us turn to Exodus chapter 1 and from that 15th verse "the king of Egypt spake to the Hebrew midwives...and he said, when ye do the office of a midwife to the Hebrew women, and see them upon the stools; if it be a son, then ye shall kill him: but if it be a daughter then she shall live." Here we have non other than Pharaoh himself coming to deliver his murderous message to these Hebrew women, "if the child being born is male, it shall die by your hand, if it is female,

then let her live." This was the edict, this was the command, and this was now the law of the land! Remember God himself had set up Pharaoh (as Romans 13 tells us). The Lord had raised up Egypt; this nation and its authorities were all instituted by the God himself, the scriptures tell us that plainly. So what of defying the kings commands!? Would these women be in a position of rebellion against God and have to suffer as a result? But let us continue. Now we have words that should be written in gold, "but the midwives feared God, and did not as the king of Egypt had command them, but saved the men children alive." (verse 17). There are many "buts" in God's Word, and here we have another one. This "but" precludes a direct refusal of the State edict, and the reason given is because "they feared God." And might we ask why did they fear God enough to disobey on fear of their lives, simply because the Lord had said "Thou shalt not Kill." It's that simple. Here we have an incredibly important principle in the Word of God, namely God's laws always supersede man's laws. Yes, the nation States are instituted by the Lord himself and are to be obeyed, but if they bring in laws that are in direct contradiction to the scriptural testimony then it is upon the scriptures we must stand, not the law of the land. The truth is that not all nation States function or act in a godly manner, and often-times head in a completely different direction, even against God and his people. In this situation:

The State Declared: Kill the Male Children.
God says "Thou Shalt not Kill" (Exodus 20:13)

Daniel, Shadrach, Meschech and Abednigo
Please turn to Daniel chapter 3 and chapter 6:1-23. Here we have two very famous passages that have gripped many a child and adult alike: The Fiery Furnace and The Lions Den. In both of these passages we learn the importance of standing for God with bravery and with boldness whatever the consequences. Again we ask, are these passages used for exciting Sunday

morning sermons to "tickle the ears" or are the real practical lessons that we should draw from these passages completely lost on the modern Christian and the leadership? We all know the stories. In chapter 3 they were told to bow down to the great image and idol of the king or be thrown into the fiery furnace. The law had gone out, the State decree had been pronounced, all that remained was obedience or face the consequences. Shadrach, Meschech and Abednigo refused, disobeyed and defied the kings command and first declared "O Nebuchadnezzar, we are not careful to answer thee in this matter." Let me just stop there, this was their first response "this thing is not up for discussion, we are not here to debate this issue, we do not need to justify our position or defend ourselves, we have no need to answer you O king." This is how they began! And they continued "...be it known unto thee, O king, that we will not serve thy gods, nor worship the golden image which thou hast set up." (verses 16-18). Again this is just so simple, the laws of God completely made void the edicts of the State when they stand in contradiction to each other. The Christian nor the Christian church is simply not bound at all to any commands that contradict or are in direct opposition to the laws of Christ and the revealed will of God for us personally or corporately.

The State Declared: Worship the Image.
God says "Thou shalt not make any graven image...Thou shalt not bow thyself down to them, nor serve them." (Exodus 20: 4-5)

Daniels Disobedience

In that 6th chapter of Daniel verses 1-23 we have the story of Daniel in the lions den and the reasons for his being thrown therein. A State edict had gone out through the manipulation of Daniels enemies. Nobody was allowed to worship any God for a period of 30 days (verse 7). Daniel openly refused and rejected the edict and when the time came "he went to his house, and his windows being open...he kneeled upon his knees three times a day, and prayed and gave thanks before his God, as he did aforetime." (verse 10) I just don't know what the pastors of our churches didn't understand about the governments regulations to shut up the churches, stop praying and stop worshipping God together, and how it is in direct contradiction to the clear revealed will of God, whether there is a pandemic or not; whether there is a war or not; whether there is a famine or any other global catastrophe or not. The point here is that it is not up to the government to 'make that call'. We are not subject to the government decrees over the house of God. It isn't in their remit to make that decision. In fact the leaders and pastors should be telling the government what to do, not the other way around. The church should be bringing to bear the responsibilities of secular leaders before a God who has put them in that position. They are to rule in righteousness, this is another simple teaching lost upon today's snowflake pastors. God has indeed raised up the secular leaders who have a biblical responsibility to be faithful, godly and righteous in the administration of their duties, and it is the preachers job to let them know their responsibilities before the Lord. But, perhaps that is another subject for another day. Here in our passage Daniel wavered not from his former customs and from his daily devotions, the edict meant nothing, as did the threats of his enemies. How far we have fallen from our former boldness and bravery of a distant bygone age. How embarrassing to capitulate at this first hurdle when no doubt more fearful and terrible times await the church in the coming tribulation. May God truly open our eyes, grant us repentance and embolden us for future days.

The State Declared: Do Not Pray or Worship any God for 30 days.

God says "worship the Lord in the beauty of his holiness." and "pray without ceasing" (Psalm 29:2) and (1 Thessalonians 5:17)

Peter and the Apostles
Not wishing to labour the point it would be remiss of me in failing to mention two scriptures from the book of Acts involving Peter and the apostles. Please look up Acts 4:1-20 and chapter 5:25-32. Remember we are talking of those who had not that long ago denied the Lord, fled at Jesus' arrest and hid away after his death upon the cross. Maybe this is a word to those pastors of our day who fear what men can do to them. To give a simple overview from those texts, the authorities took hold of Peter and John as they were preaching and they actually put them in prison. The decree then went out from these God-ordained leaders with the power of life and death in their hands, again leaders directly set up and instituted by God himself, but they abused their power and "killed the prince of life," (Acts 3:15) and could quite easily take away the apostles lives with just a word and a sentence. Instead they beat them up and "commanded them not to speak at all, nor teach in the name of Jesus." (chapter 4:18) How did that go with the apostles!? If ever there was an authority set up by the Lord, surely this was it: the religious leaders of the day and boy did they know their scriptures! "whether it be right in the sight of God to hearken unto you more than unto God, judge ye. For we cannot but speak the things we have seen and heard." (verses 19-20) and again when questioned further on this matter in chapter 5:29 "Peter and the other apostles answered, and said, we ought to obey God rather then men." Even these illustrious church leaders and their edicts and commands were to be rejected completely because the command of Christ had already gone out and their extra rules contradicted the Lords word.

The State Declared: Do Not Teach or Preach in Jesus' Name. God says "Preach the word..." and again "Go and stand and speak...to the people all the words of this life." (2 Timothy 4:1-2) and (Acts 5:20)

Conclusion

I have not sought to exegete these passages only give a simple overview to make the point that when any ruler anywhere dares to make and enforce laws which are in direct conflict with the revealed will of God for our lives and the functionality of our corporate gatherings, then we stand on biblical ground to make a wholesale rejection of those decrees whatever the consequences might be. The statutes of our God always supersede, nullify and make void those unrighteous demands and commands by governments, Kings, Queens, Church authorities, Magistrates etc. whether local, national, international and global. We are not bound to obey and we are truly free to disobey with clear consciences to the great glory of our God and our true King Jesus Christ. Whilst we do indeed seek to be good citizens wherever we may dwell, praying for those that God has put over us, we also seek the blessing of the State and it's people and this we achieve by evangelising the lost which we know from time to time shall bring us into conflict with the Law. Do we stop? Do we hide? Do we forsake that true biblical preaching of the whole counsel of God? Do we close our churches and gatherings, whether we meet openly and freely or whether in secret? In short do we capitulate?

Covid-19 has shown beyond a shadow of doubt that the church universal has already removed those ancient boundary stones and foundational Christian truths simply because it had no fight whatsoever, and it had nothing to fight with. It looked out at the Covid world created by our governments and saw the fear engendered, the political lies, the healthcare deceptions; it saw the mass medical paranoia and hysteria; it saw the government crackdowns and heavy handed police tactics, the millions of lost businesses; it looked at the growing mental health crises; it saw the alternative medical opinions from experts in their relative fields completely shut down; it looked at the new laws created to keep everybody under some type of house arrest, laws that shut down the whole economy, and laws that even shut down our churches; it looked out at all this and thought absolutely nothing. The church had nothing to offer apart from "Zoom." The overwhelming majority of church leaders thought that all of the above mentioned things were OK, they were fine, they were justified, they were righteous. The governments were doing the best that they could given a tough situation. It was a question of "nothing to see here, lets just keep quiet for two years and move on." No research, no study, no pleading the Lord for insight, for truth or reality; no sermons to strengthen their congregations bombarded by fear and lies, all masked up like frightened little children. There were no protests and no preaching directly at our government officials making them accountable before God.

Many of our congregations might appear sound biblical churches, and many might like to think that they are building upon a rock, but Covid blew away their delusions and exposed their cowardice, compliance and acquiescence. The so called Covid-19 crises was just a for runner of what is to come. It cannot be denied that the church believed and obeyed every single word of our governments, this a simple fact. You must do this, you must do that, you must take the vaccine. Ask yourself, what if the government asked you to be micro chipped, or to take some type of mark to be able to buy or sell, and it was all wrapped up in similar language used in the Covid crises, would you take it? What makes you think that you wouldn't when you've already given in and when you've already been fooled and totally hoodwinked? Where do you think that you are going to get your strength from when you've already moved the foundations, and when the edifice of your life or church is built upon sand? These are very real questions that must be answered, yes they are disturbing and searching questions but if we have any sense of honour to our God and the sheep that the Lord might have put in our care we must answer them. Don't be too proud to do a bit of self examination as mentioned in a previous chapter.

Let me add here that I am not saying that these are easy decisions to make. I understand completely that Covid-19 and the subsequent government impositions are a unique situation which the majority of us have never been faced with before. I also understand that many pastors have been well meaning in their approach and have struggled to find a balance between what they know in their conscience is wrong i.e. the closing of the churches, and a fearful, brainwashed flock subjected to a daily diet of lies, deception and fear tactics by the media and the government. I know that it has been difficult to navigate through such choppy waters, and there would have been different reasons for different reactions among the differing congregations. I understand also that there were strong opinions in all our churches, but that does not mean that the truth cannot be understood and that lies cannot be exposed. I have only sought to bring to bear certain questions and made certain conclusions if certain leaders have reacted in certain ways. Anyone reading these words can only be honest and say "yes, that's me, or no, that's not me."

In making the decisions that you made did you involve the whole congregation or did you make an arbitrary decision based upon your own personal fear? Did you gain the full support of the whole congregation in keeping the doors open despite the new laws? Or was the church not even consulted and the doors closed? Did you appeal for support from the congregation if you were to make a biblical stand should you be fined or arrested? Or did you not even 'go there' really fearing that a police record might cost you your job, career and respect amongst your unbelieving peers? Did you really pray about Romans 13 and its true meaning and application, seeking God's guidance? Or had you already made your mind up that the state has to be obeyed in all situations and at all times, including the functioning of all things ecclesiastical? Did you do any real research at all, trying to get to the truthfulness or otherwise of the pandemic? Or was it of no real concern what people were experiencing, what fears they had imbibed, or what abject hysteria and madness had engulfed the dear flock of Christ? Was this manufactured by man? Or was this the judgement of God? Either way did you really care for the answer?

Remember this was an actual global crises, everything and everybody was affected upon the entire globe, for it to be of no concern (if that was the case) then one thing is for sure you are in the wrong job. You alone can answer such questions honestly, and give reason why you made the decisions that you did, one way or the other. It is to the Lord himself that that account must be given to, not me. All I know is that even people in the world have shown more bravery in defying those who would try and keep them from a dying relative, or from enjoying a normal (God-Ordained) family experience. I fear that worse things are to come, as I have alluded to. When the powers of hell are unleashed and when the roaring lion is given free rein to do his worst, how then shall we bear up? How shall we fare then in the great tribulation when here and now a virus akin to the flu with the overwhelming majority of people experiencing very mild cold-like symptoms (if any at all) completely decimates and destroys our Christian testimony?

Apologia and Final Thoughts

Covid-19 became an issue of global concern whilst I was writing this little book, and as I have alluded to, I see it now as providentially feeding into the narrative and wider context of what I have been attempting to put forward. I also see it as a kind of vindication of what I have been suggesting in this book. If I had any doubts then they have been completely dispelled. Who am I to say such things? What credentials do I hold? Who do I think that I am claiming to see the mind and will of God whilst our leadership sees nothing? What displays of arrogance and bigotry; what terrible words I've used; how judgemental, hard-hearted and sometimes even cruel. How disrespectful to speak of men of much higher standing and learning; how dare you "lay your hands upon the Lord's anointed" in this ignorant and arrogant way. These are the words that I have already heard from individual Christians and church leaders. However, I have sought to speak from the heart to the heart that which 30 years of walking with the Lord has burdened me with. As I said right at the beginning, I am no academic (well that's pretty obvious some might say) but God has placed a burden upon me, and these words are just some of that burden. Here let me also add that I am speaking from a position of failure and fear myself. I know all about acquiescence to intimidation, cowardice gripping the soul and paralysing my spiritual life. You have to believe me also that I know just exactly what it is to hurt, to offend and to harm people, and I know experimentally of catastrophic falls. I do not make personal judgements about people as some falsely accuse, but I do make a judgement based upon truth and what I observe in the churches through that particular lens. Remember, Peter who denied the Lord, could himself accuse his fellow countrymen of the same sin without conflict of conscience or charges of hypocrisy, "...ye delivered up, and *denied* him in the presence of Pilate, when he was determined to let him go, but ye *denied* The Holy One..." (Acts 3:13-14). "Hang on a minute Peter, *you* did the same, *you* denied your

Lord three times, even with oaths and curses, who are you to accuse others, is this not just rank hypocrisy?" This is where grace, and love, and mercy is seen in its highest and purest form. I thought all the Christian leaders knew and believed this, and even experienced this grace; now I'm not so sure. Peter wept bitterly and repented of his fall, and thus a risen Christ forgives him completely, and cleanses him thoroughly. I myself speak from this very same standpoint: a sinner saved by grace alone, and restored by divine love.

We're All 'Snowflakes' Now?

The world is changing and has always changed, culture moves and fluctuates; it goes up to higher levels and can easily drop into the gutter. We are heading for the gutter. The Judeo-Christian culture is fading and the Post-Truth world is enveloping us all. The society is turning into a kind of 'liberal fascism' which can be defined as allowing everybody to live just exactly how they desire to live but no one is allowed to disagree with it. The concepts of agreeing-to-disagree and making informed choices formed out of robust and vigorous debate etc. is almost completely gone. The age of 'cancel culture' is upon us. This evil can be seen every day almost everywhere we look, lives totally destroyed for having an alternative opinion, a different world-view, people guilty of "wrong-think" and "thought-crimes". The most disturbing thing about this intellectual narcissistic hysteria is that it is being protected by law all over the world in the form of what is known as "hate speech laws" and "hate crime laws," To actually say or even think the 'wrong' thing is becoming a crime, to offend somebody else's feelings by your own world-view, opinions and/or alternative narrative is actually becoming illegal! And if it is not yet a crime, it is regarded as something very close to it in the form of company 'policies and procedures' and 'company values', and anyone falling foul of these 'values' will find a hard time keeping their job. Such in-house rules gives offended minority groups and managers free reign to crush anybody they wish that doesn't hold to the said 'values', "think like we do and believe what we do or else!" This is the societal back-ground of this book and the thinking behind it. The Christian, the Church and our very existence is most definitely under threat, and I have come to realise and understand that just to be a Christian in this 'liberal-fascism' culture and context is to be in conflict almost every single day. The policies and procedures of most of our institutions are laced right through with this thinking and it creates conflict and frustration because it cuts right across everything that is true, honest and just, whilst at the same time speaking of inclusion and well-being. See what happens if you don't toe-the-line and dare to speak up at one of their little seminars or 'zoom meetings' on equality and diversity or institutionalised racism. The whole system is creating less inclusion, less diversity, less real choice and much more genuine discrimination. It is the church of Jesus Christ alone that can offer, and does actually bring into peoples lives a true equality in its very real diversity.

There is a fight back (in the world that is!) amongst a number of people, some of whom who's voices are stronger than others, but even now plans are afoot to shut down the avenues of freedom of expression and free thought. The world's governments have sought, and are now actively working to bring their hate crime laws, with their pretended offence caused, their manufactured hurt and perceived harm into the on-line world, this is with the complete backing of the internet giants, big tech, social and mainstream media etc. Like I said there are voices of dissent and there does appear an awakening of some sort as-it-were. People are not happy with their ever intrusive work environments, of the lies they are told everyday by mainstream media, of the 'cancel culture', of being told what to think, how to behave and how they must live. People feel a type of out-of-syncness with themselves and the world. They know that something is just not quite right, and they believe that something nefarious is going on on a global scale, and that their own particular individualism is being sucked up into a kind of trans-human multi-verse, and there isn't much they can do about it. There are however many more millions of people who just couldn't care less and cannot see anything of what I speak. They just brush it all off and are carry on with the global flow and direction of those who tell them where to go, what to do and what to think, as long as they get their fix of leisure, pleasure, porn, drink and drugs, they really couldn't care less.

Of all people upon the earth, it is the Christian community which should see all this going on and who should be resisting, fighting and speaking loudly directly into our current societal context. We of all people should have the answers, the insight, the comfort and "the Truth". Indeed we do have the answers, or I should say our God and saviour has all the answers to any of our situations in this lost world. Being born-again by God's Holy Spirit, 'seeing-the-light', repenting of our sins and believing upon a risen Christ is the ultimate 'Red Pill' experience. Our spiritual awakening can be compared to nothing else; the actual creator of the real universe revealing himself to us personally and inwardly far outweighs any meta-verse experience, and what's more, it's real and not fake. Friends and brethren in Christ, we should have been an answer in our world but we are blinded by it all just like the world itself. The simple ancient boundaries I have been exhorting to have been removed and we haven't really understood the dangers, but it was all revealed when Covid-19 came along, because the church had nothing to offer and just closed their doors, took the vaccines and saw nothing, absolutely nothing. The foundations of our testimony were already destroyed, the decay was already set in despite us all going to church, enjoying our activities and then going home to our little lives. The vision and the fight is being waged by those who don't even believe in God, or the bible or in Jesus as saviour, and they don't even fully realise what the fight is all about, like I said they know something is wrong and are fighting when and where they can. We know that "the old serpent, called the Devil, and Satan, which deceiveth the whole world," that "he was cast out into the earth, and his angels were cast out with him," (Revelation 12:9) that it is he and his evil hordes destroying everything and everyone he can get his hands upon for he knows his time is short and he has great wrath. (Revelation 12:12). What we are seeing now unfolding before our very eyes is the devil and his disciples upon the earth in all those positions of global power and authority preparing the way for the coming Anti-Christ. I see this as plain as the sun in the sky, but I fear that the leaders of our churches see nothing at all.

We hold our conferences and sing our songs etc. We know our bibles and all the stories therein which are supposed to breathe living faith into the soul. We've all read of the hero's of faith in Hebrews chapter 11, and like I've mentioned throughout this book we've read of many other powerful examples for us to follow and emulate. Many Christian leaders no doubt know their Christian history, the early church martyrs, those burned at the stake, imprisoned and tortured. Untold bravery is everywhere within the Christian Faith throughout two thousand years of recorded testimony, and yet knowing all this we make such pathetic excuses and unbiblical appeals to Romans 13 to justify our cowardice when we should be building again the foundations, the walls and the Temple; when we should be restoring that which has been rejected and denied. When also we should be getting back into the hands of our people a reliable translation of the scriptures before it becomes an archaeological relic; when we should be preaching again (without fear or compromise) the whole counsel of God and raising the bar of biblical truth by holding forth the whole of the Word of God, which has been miraculously preserved in the Old and New Testaments. When we should be examining our walk before God and setting things right and getting back our zeal, our fight and back-bone for the war that is to be unleashed upon the earth, realising and understanding that we too might have to become law-breakers and enemies of the State. They who preach and live properly before the Lord 'will' know conflict as night follows day, it will happen, it will come. Paul tells Timothy plainly "...all that will live godly in Christ Jesus shall suffer persecution." (2 Timothy 3:12). Drop that in your promise box! It came upon Moses, it came to Samuel, it came to David, it came to the Prophets, it came to John the Baptist, it came upon the disciples and apostles of our Lord, and came to our Lord Jesus himself. It has also come upon all those Christian communities throughout two millennia of church history, why should we be any different? Why would we expect it to be different for us? It will only be different for us, and we shall know no persecution and conflict because we have nothing to offer, it's as simple as that, our message might appear sound but it lacks something: Application and Power. We have filtered biblical truth through the sieve of fear and compromise and are left with a much more watered down message than we realise.

Too Late to Change?
My final appeal dear brethren, is for any who read these words to not be too offended. If I could beg you I would. Instead I appeal to the scriptures, Solomon tells us that "open rebuke is better than secret love. Faithful are the wounds of a friend; but the kisses of the enemy are deceitful." (Proverbs 27:5-6). What I speak here is truth, beware the "it's all about love" mentality, because it isn't, it's false, it's a lie. Judas betrayed our Lord with a kiss, and my love extends to all in my rebukes and wounds, I mean no one any ill will. I ask any who read these words to be honest and look into these things. I would ask you to take a moment, take some 'time out' to seek the Lord to see if these things are right. I would urge you to look at four things honestly and with an open heart.

Firstly, look out at the world, do some research, educate yourself as to what is really going on. Behold the lies, the deceptions, the manipulation of the entire world and see what real influence "the god of this world" really has. (2 Corinthians 4:4). Which way is the wind blowing? Do you see a world that is being influenced by Christian truth? Or is it becoming more depraved and duplicitous by the second? Do you see order forming? Or do you see chaos, confusion and lies, "the sons of Belial" gaining more and more power? In our homes, lives, communities and work environments, do you see harmony and peace? Or do you see 'dog-eat-dog', misery, sorrow and brokenness? Do you see a rise in Christian principles or a rise in the occult? Do you see our governments acting with honour or dishonour? Do they act in their own nations citizens interest, their own personal interest, or in the interest of the elite globalists? In this situation it is the children of the world who are wiser than the children of God, but this should not be the case. Look at the world.

Secondly, I would ask that you would look at the Church of Jesus Christ. In Ezekiel chapter 8 we have the story of God asking the Prophet to make a hole in the wall and to go through the door to see what is going on within the "house of Israel." Look for yourself, be honest, open your eyes, look at the blasphemous mega churches reaping the rewards of the manipulated sheep, lining the pockets of those millionaire pastors with their multiple houses, and cars and private jets. And I am not only speaking of the prosperity gospel pedlars. Many of our so-called heroes, who's study bibles we have on our shelves, whom we admire, who also we have found a great blessing; they too have multi-million dollar homes, numerous cars, swimming pools, tennis courts etc. Even their lifestyles are a complete affront to biblical Christianity. Look also at our own smaller churches removing the ancient boundary stones that the Lord himself has laid and casting off the fundamentals of the Faith, some in more subtle ways than others. These same smaller churches imbibe the same mentality as the bigger ones. Quite often the 'money-god' or the 'careerer-god' reigns and anything that threatens these things is compromised upon. Covid regulations proved that one! I have moved in smaller church circles myself, I would ask you to start asking people where they stand on a whole host of biblical fundamentals, and you will find that you will get a whole host of different answers. The creation, the fall, the flood, the covenants of God, the wars, the judgements, the cross-work of Christ, the miracles, God's salvation, the end times, heaven and hell etc. etc. Non of it seems to matter, it doesn't seem to matter what one believes; and as I mentioned in an earlier study the 'grey areas' of points not deemed necessary for salvation is getting wider and wider. If you think that there is uniformity, then think again. Look at the Church.

Thirdly, look into your own heart. This has been the appeal of these pages and the urgent cry of *my* own heart. In the final analysis I cannot see or read the heart, I can only ask questions. Brethren, in the light of what I have been trying to say ask yourself your own questions, honestly and prayerfully. Look into your heart.

Fourthly, look up to the God of your salvation "humble yourself under the mighty hand of God, that he may exalt you in due time." (1 Peter 5:6). Don't look at the messenger, rather look at the message and the God of the message. I urge you to be as "the children of Issachar, which were men that had understanding of the times, to know what Israel ought to do..." (1 Chronicles 12:32). This would suggest that it is quite possible to not have understanding of the times to know what the church should doing. It is more than possible to be totally blind to the days in which we live. To have "understanding of the times" isn't about having knowledge of church history or Christian theology, it's about having spiritual discernment. It's about knowing what what God wants and seeing what God sees, not what the latest high-flying multi-millionaire Pastor says from some American Mega Church. Much of these men's work (in my opinion) will be burned up, it is wood, hay and stubble. Look up to God.

Let us however return to the God of our salvation and seek to be building upon the rock, that solid foundational, biblical, evangelical, protestant, life-transforming, heart-warming, soul-saving Christianity, fearing nothing and no one, but God and sin. Amen.

"Ye shall know the truth, and the truth shall make you free."
(John 8:32).

If you have found this book a blessing then please feel free to leave just a couple of sentences of a positive review on Amazon. This would be really helpful regarding other potential readers and also how Amazon recommendations work. I am also more than willing and open to constructive criticism. Thank you.

If you have found some of these issues challenging or think them even wrong then let "iron sharpen iron" and please contact me personally at: deanstevenson367@talktalk.net and lets have a chat!

Thank you for purchasing and reading this little offering, and may the Lord Jesus Christ bless your eternal soul with every spiritual blessing in Christ, and that:

"...the God of our Lord Jesus Christ, the Father of glory, may give unto the Spirit of wisdom and revelation in the knowledge of him: The eyes of your understanding being enlightened; that ye may know what is the hope of his calling, and what the riches of the glory of his inheritance in the saints, and what is the exceeding greatness of his power to usward who believe, according to the working of his mighty power, which he wrought in Christ, when he raised him from the dead..." (Ephesians 1:17-20)

Printed in Great Britain
by Amazon